Teaming to Innovate

Jossey-Bass Short Format Series

Written by thought leaders and experts in their fields, pieces in the Jossey-Bass Short Format Series provide busy, on-the-go professionals, managers, and leaders around the world with must-have, just-in-time information in a concise and actionable format.

To learn more, visit www.josseybass.com/go/shortform

Also by Amy C. Edmondson

Teaming: How Organizations Learn, Innovate, and Compete in the Knowledge Economy

Teaming to Innovate

AMY C. EDMONDSON

JB JOSSEY-BASS™

A Wiley Brand

Jossey-Bass books and products are available through most bookstores. To contact Jossey-Bass directly call our Customer Care Department within the U.S. at 800-956-7739, outside the U.S. at 317-572-3986, or fax 317-572-4002.

Wiley publishes in a variety of print and electronic formats and by print-on-demand. Some material included with standard print versions of this book may not be included in e-books or in print-on-demand. If this book refers to media such as a CD or DVD that is not included in the version you purchased, you may download this material at http://booksupport.wiley.com. For more information about Wiley products, visit www.wiley.com.

ISBN 978-1-118-85627-7 (paper); ISBN 978-1-118-78827-1 (ePDF);
ISBN 978-1-118-78843-1 (ePub)

FIRST EDITION

SKY10052193_072823

Contents

Executive Summary

This short book is about *leadership and teaming in the context of innovation*. What is teaming? It's what happens when people collaborate—across boundaries of expertise, hierarchy, or geographic distance, to name a few. Teaming is a process of bringing together skills and ideas from disparate areas to produce something new—something that no one individual, or even a group in one area of expertise, could do alone. This is why teaming is so crucial to innovation. When teaming works, the results are more than the sum of the parts, and those who participated are inspired by what they have created and by what they have learned. In some ways, teaming to innovate is the most engaging and rewarding kind of teaming there is.

The goal of this book is to compile key insights for managers who want to lead teaming focused on innovation. I introduce new ideas and case studies from my recent research, and also draw heavily from the longer book, *Teaming*, to suggest a particular approach to leading innovation. *Teaming to Innovate* offers succinct advice and a set of memorable strategies that managers and leaders can easily keep in mind to drive innovation.

I provide a road map for *teaming to innovate*, with five essential recommendations:

1. Aim High
2. Team Up
3. Fail Well
4. Learn Fast
5. Repeat (Start all over again! Innovation takes a few iterations.)

Each of the first four recommendations is illustrated with real-life examples that show how teaming to innovate provides the spark that can clarify goals, nurture creativity, and enable synergy.

Introduction

Wherever you work, it is likely that intense competition, rampant unpredictability, and demanding customers are fueling a demand for innovation. But simply calling for innovation isn't enough to produce it.

What It Takes to Innovate

The ability to develop creative, viable, new products or services that solve a problem or serve a need, and do so profitably, requires: teamwork, an organizational culture that embraces paradox, and an unusual leadership mind-set.

Teamwork

Innovation thrives when people from different disciplines and backgrounds come together to develop new possibilities that none of them could have envisioned alone. Making this happen requires that diverse individuals work exceedingly well together. Rather than just bringing their expertise, ideas, and biases to a project and tossing them into the mix, groups that end up innovating effectively find ways to roll up their sleeves and work together. They find ways to genuinely integrate their different perspectives so as to create brand-new possibilities. This is teaming.

Why call it teaming, rather than simply the creation of an effective team? Because innovation is a fluid process and follows an uncertain course. This means that it is not always possible to know in advance exactly what skills you'll need on a team or how long you'll need them, making it difficult to plan and build a stable, well-designed team before the job gets under way.

In a typical hospital emergency room, for example, patient outcomes depend upon seamless coordination and superb communication among diverse clinicians who may not even know each other's names at the outset of the encounter. That's teaming. High-quality teaming blends getting to know people quickly—their knowledge, skills, and goals—with listening to other points of view, coordinating actions, and making shared decisions.

Effective teaming happens when everyone remains highly aware of others' needs, roles, and perspectives. This entails learning to relate to people who are different and learning to integrate different perspectives into new, shared possibilities, plans, and actions. Doing this well requires both affective (feeling) and cognitive (thinking) skills. It also requires leadership (more on this below). When it's done well, teaming for innovation leads to new processes, products, and services that make the organization more valuable and those it serves better off.[1]

The core message of this book is that today's business leaders need to understand and nurture this process of *teaming for innovation* to ensure the future success of the enterprise.

A Culture of Paradox

Innovative organizations tend to have cultures that embrace paradox. This is because innovation depends upon the coexistence of pairs of seeming opposites: play and discipline; high standards and a tolerance for failure;

the use of deep experts and boundary-spanning general-ists who deeply empathize with customers.

Playful chaos and focused discipline. Organizations that innovate, whether to invent a new business model, come up with a new product, or improve a process, know how to focus on an important problem. At the same time, innovation is an all-too-human process—inherently unpredictable and often chaotic. If you want to innovate, any idea has to be welcome, at least early on before ideas are winnowed down. But welcoming all ideas, "wacky" ones included, creates a sense of chaos.

The key is asking good questions—and not know-ing the answer in advance! Franck Riboud is CEO of Groupe Danone, a creative and purposeful consumer goods company (best known for its yogurt) that has reinvented itself many times throughout its 94-year his-tory. He welcomes the chaos of not knowing in advance what employees will come up with. In an interview for a Harvard Business School case study, he said:

> It's like a Lego box that you buy for your chil-dren. They start to play, trying to find a way to build the image on the Lego box. At the end of the day, they give up, throw out the box, and put the pieces away. The next weekend you put

all the Lego pieces on the floor and then they try to imagine something. Not what was on the box, but what they have in their heads.[2]

To Riboud, strategy happens when employees come up with something new, not when they follow the instruction manual.

Known for its success in product development, IDEO, the design firm, has received media attention for its freewheeling idea-generation, a process which gradually narrows in on compelling solutions for customers. The company deviates dramatically from the cubicle culture dominating modern workplaces, where people's tasks are highly constrained. IDEO exudes playfulness, complete with a "tech box" full of odd objects for triggering associations, patterns, and ideas. The firm deliberately hires across an array of disciplines—putting people of differing backgrounds, who look at situations from varying angles, together in project teams.[3]

IDEO's approach to product innovation emphasizes collaboration in multidisciplinary teams, fresh thinking, and empathic devotion to user needs. But it also involves a disciplined process. For all the exploration and experimentation, each stage of this process has "deliverables," and a concrete, results-oriented mentality is at work.

Deep experts and broad thinkers. Innovation happens when diverse experts (in a specific topic, subject area, or clinical specialty, for instance) and broad, general thinkers come together. The generalists keep their eye on the ball, on the goal—something that has usually never been done before. Without them, the specialists can get mired in the past, convinced of what has previously been possible, or impossible. But the generalists lack the depth and practicality of the specialists' experience (technical, procedural, even emotional).

Lake Nona Medical City is a 7,000-acre residential and research cluster in Central Florida.[4] The idea for this living laboratory was spearheaded by Tavistock Group, a private investment organization. The project aimed to develop an innovation cluster, complete with a master planned community, focused on biomedical research, clinical care, and medical education in a healthy, eco-friendly environment. Tavistock founded Lake Nona Property Holdings to develop the community and the nonprofit Lake Nona Institute to support the mission. By 2012, a diverse group of partners had moved onto plots of land at the development.

To realize the community's ambitious goals, Thad Seymour, president of the Lake Nona Institute, knew that he would have to work effectively with a growing roster of partners across sectors and industries. Rather than hiring traditional developers, Tavistock's leaders staffed Lake Nona Property Holdings and the Lake Nona Institute with executives from a variety of backgrounds, each bringing an area of expertise that reflected one or more of four pillars: sustainability, technology, health and wellness, and education.

The success of the project was summarized in a speech by City of Orlando mayor Buddy Dyer in February 2012:

> Realizing that we would not be able to compete for companies and jobs of the future unless we redefined the way our entire region worked together, this community committed itself to a level of cooperation never before seen in Central Florida. In fostering the partnership necessary to create the Medical City, we didn't just build a one-time project. We also created a road map for how to get big, important things done and how to overcome the challenges that confront our community.[5]

Many in the Lake Nona project pointed to the role of the institute's culture in promoting innovation. To encourage innovation, Lake Nona's leaders had followed an unusual approach for real estate development. Leaders of the various tenant organizations described Lake Nona as an "accelerator," a "manager," an "engineer," a "conductor," and a "builder of collaboration." The Lake Nona team's strategy, they stressed, was to encourage innovation by investing in collaboration.

High standards and high failure tolerance. Innovation happens when the organization's culture promotes high standards and high tolerance of failure at the same time. That sounds wrong at first, but in fact it's sensible. Innovation requires iteration. It requires drive and ambition, but also accepting that you'll almost never get it right the first time. And spreading successful innovation in a large organization requires finding ways to shine a quiet spotlight on innovators so that others are drawn to try it, too.

The technology company 3M has earned a reputation for successful product innovation by encouraging deliberate experimentation and by cultivating a culture that is tolerant, even rewarding of failures. Failures are seen as a necessary step in a larger process of developing successful, innovative products. Apocryphal stories such as that of Arthur Fry and the failed super-adhesive that spawned the Post-it note industry are spread far and wide, both within and outside the company. Setting goals, such as that of having 25 percent of a division's revenues come from products introduced within the last five years, means that divisions must be actively experimenting to develop new products.[6]

An Unusual Leadership Mind-set

In any successful organization, leadership exercises three basic levers that influence the actions of others. The *first* is communicating an inspiring picture of a desirable future. Whether you think of it as a vision or a compelling shared goal, this future-oriented communication is designed to inspire and motivate others to go further than they would ordinarily go. The *second* lever is modeling desired behaviors. Those in positions of power and status are watched closely. In that way, what leaders do powerfully influences what others do. The *third* is direct coaching and feedback, which help individuals and teams develop into great producers and leaders themselves.

Routinely engaging in these activities is how people develop themselves as leaders while also helping the organization carry out its mission. But it won't happen without commitment and cultural support. Moreover, leading innovation is tricky because of innovation's apparently contradictory qualities.

Leaders who want to foster innovation have to *promote and model contradictory attitudes and actions*. They live with paradox. As we've seen above with organizational culture, a leader's role in fostering innovation is to build a culture that is playful and disciplined; chaotic and focused; full of experts and broad-thinking boundary-spanners; a culture that promotes high standards and tolerates failure. A culture of possibility.

Before we look at how that culture is created and nurtured, let's take a look at the various contexts in which innovation is called for, and what sets it apart from other contexts. As a way to organize our thinking about these contexts (the difference, say, between a fast-food restaurant and a hospital), consider the Process Knowledge Spectrum.[7] Failure means something different in each of these contexts. The same is true for collaboration, relationships, learning, and creativity.

Situating Innovation on the Process Knowledge Spectrum

By "process knowledge," I mean knowledge about how to produce a desired result, whether a laptop, a hamburger, or a successful surgery. The more knowledge we have about how to achieve a particular outcome—for instance, how to manufacture an automobile or mend a broken arm—the more mature the knowledge. The less knowledge we have about how something is done—for example, how to create an affordable car with no carbon footprint—the less mature the knowledge. When process knowledge is well developed or mature, as in a manufacturing setting, uncertainty is low. The Process Knowledge Spectrum, elaborated in Table 1 for different kinds of organizations, characterizes work according to how much knowledge we have about translating goals into results, and how well we understand the relationships between cause and effect.[8]

At one end of the Process Knowledge Spectrum we find high-volume, repetitive work, such as you might see in fast-food restaurants, call centers, or assembly plants. At the other end is research and discovery. Because prior experience achieving a desired goal is limited, making progress requires risk-taking and experimentation. In the middle are complex operations, exemplified by complex service organizations like a tertiary-care hospital, where some knowledge is mature, such as the procedure for drawing blood, but much knowledge, like how to treat a rare disease or the mix of patients to expect on any given

Table 1. How Single Organizations Encompass Routine, Complex, and Innovation Operations

	Routine Operations	Complex Operations	Innovation Operations
Automotive company	Assembly plant	Supply chain management	Design and development of future cars
Computer chip maker	Fabrication plant	Supply chain management	Design and development of next-generation chips
Personal computer company	Assembly plant	Support and service for large-business customers	Design and development of future computing devices
Fast-food company	Restaurants	Supply chain management	Research and development of future products and services
University	Dormitory management	Building construction project	Research labs, curriculum redesign group
Space exploration agency	Payroll operations	Space missions	Developing future programs
Airport	Security, food services	Air traffic control	Future planning
Hospital	Phlebotomy	Emergency room	Electronic medical record implementation

day, is unknown or in flux. In these settings, teaming is challenging. But it is also invaluable.

Routine Operations

Laptops, toasters, or cars: every assembly plant relies on and applies well-developed and precisely codified process knowledge. There is no room for uncertainty. Learning is largely focused on improvement and making existing processes more accurate, less expensive, and less time-consuming. In short, success equals improved efficiency.

But even routine operations don't hum along forever. New machinery and new products often require temporary problem solving to develop new processes that will soon become standardized. Once the problems are solved and the bumps and hiccups removed, new standards and scripts can be devised. New products or services then become routine. The transition period is limited. Teaming and organizing to learn are integral to the process of organizing to execute.

Complex Operations

Uncertainty about arrival times, customer-specific needs, and unpredictable interactions make complex operations challenging to manage. Although knowledge of how to produce most of the specific results exists in a reasonably mature state for some, many situations can be difficult to predict. The combination of tasks is constantly shifting. Often, old and new tasks interact to produce novel, unexpected, or problematic results.

Learning in this context is largely about solving process problems—disruptions that impede task completion, often due to shortages of material, skill, or time, or to other sources of interference.[9] But complex organizations also confront larger problems and more compelling challenges, such as safely operating a nuclear power plant or managing a space exploration program. Learning may involve collecting data to better understand patterns of customer arrival and need, increasing predictability, and designing less chaotic operations. Nonetheless, it is impossible to remove all uncertainty from complex operations! Perpetual problem solving is a way of life in these settings.

Innovation Operations

In innovation operations, the primary purpose is to experiment and generate new possibilities that can be taken all the way to the market or that solve an organizational or a social problem. Successful innovation always works with novelty. Innovating, whether in product development or problem solving, means working without a blueprint.

Innovation operations often have vague, if ambitious, goals that require experimentation, trial and error, and collective brainstorming to achieve. Designers, engineers, marketers, and researchers actively and continually learn in order to come up with new products and services that keep their companies competitive. The team boundaries may be porous. Individuals may join and leave the project at different points during the process, and roles for individual team members may shift as the project progresses. Many tasks must be defined, assigned, and improvised on the go. The work requires constant learning to create new possibilities. Because of the uncertainty of the innovation process, failure is frequent along the way, and expected. Acceptable failure rates for research-based enterprises like biotechnology corporations may be well over 90 percent.

Encompassing the Full Spectrum

Most organizations—certainly most large organizations—encompass all three types of operations. Consider Toyota. Its famously efficient assembly plants epitomize the activity most people associate with a car company, namely routine operations. Does that mean Toyota only plays in the routine operations space? Not even close. A complex global company like Toyota necessarily encompasses complex and innovation operations as well.[10]

Toyota has a large and vibrant R&D organization, one that developed the first widely available hybrid (electric- and gasoline-powered) vehicle, the *Prius*, giving Toyota an innovative, desirable "green" vehicle several years before competitors. Toyota's new-product development process, like that of numerous other manufacturing companies, starts with cross-functional teaming to figure out what the product ultimately ought to be and to develop detailed specifications. Next an interconnected set of smaller teams starts solving the problems these detailed specifications create. Ultimately, the proposed new design is handed off to manufacturing. To take a cutting-edge car from concept to market requires understanding customer preferences and designing to satisfy them, figuring out which existing components to keep and teaming with parts suppliers to develop brand-new components, while also ensuring that in-house and supplier components are integrated and tested. Add to this complexity a diversity of locations, cultures, and regulatory policies, and the magnitude of the innovation challenge is clear. It should also be clear that anyone working on a new car design is doing something he or she has not done exactly the same way before. Novelty dominates the process, requiring extensive brainstorming, communication, and difficult decisions along the way, through a series of teaming encounters. And failure is not only impossible to avoid; it's an essential part of the innovation process.[11]

A Recipe for Innovation

Leaders seeking to inspire, enhance, or revive innovation in their organization often wonder what to do. They understand that just asking for innovation will not produce it. They recognize that cross-disciplinary groups do not always come up with terrific new ideas, and synergy is not a necessary outcome of collaboration across boundaries. In fact, without an unusual mix of openness, humility, talent, drive, and creativity, innovation may not occur. It is clear that leadership is needed to nurture these qualities in fluid groupings of people—often both inside and outside the organization—and channel them toward desired ends.

Teaming for innovation is dynamic. It involves identifying (often temporary) collaborators and getting up to speed quickly on what needs to be done and what role each collaborator can play. This kind of flexibility is needed more and more in workplaces across many industries. A growing portion of the work itself—whether product design, patient care, custom software, or strategic decision making—presents complicated interdependencies that often have to be managed on the fly.

But no matter how flexible and willing one's colleagues may be, effective teaming rarely happens spontaneously. It takes effort. Teaming requires letting down your guard to work interdependently with others. It requires offering your ideas and skills thoughtfully while being equally, if not more, interested in what others have to offer, no matter what their status or position in the hierarchy. It requires accepting that it's simply not possible to look good or be right all the time. Teaming to innovate requires creativity, humility, empathy, and drive. Because these attributes can wax and wane in the real world, especially in the workplace, leaders need to nurture them.

In a nutshell, the leadership task in innovation is to keep people focused on what's at stake—on the purpose the organization seeks to serve and the goals it's striving to achieve—and to be stewards of the contradictory and paradoxical culture of innovation.

Consider this little book a road map for leaders who wish to inspire or participate in the innovation journey. Each of the following sections elaborates one of four overarching recommendations for leaders seeking to enhance innovation in their organization:

1. Aim High
2. Team Up
3. Fail Well
4. Learn Fast

That's basically it. It's simple. (Note that simple doesn't mean easy!) And there is a fifth recommendation as well:

5. Repeat

The fifth recommendation is added because the need for innovation never stops, and the likelihood of failure along the way never lessens. Innovation is achieved in a continuous looping journey. "Repeat" sometimes means that a second, narrower, more focused search is underway, but it sometimes means starting at the beginning again: revisiting goals against changes that may have occurred since goals were set, teaming up with new collaborators, producing new failures, and learning again, as fast as ever.

By its nature, the innovation path is not smooth. To better understand each critical recommendation, in the pages ahead we'll look at case studies from my research in diverse organizations. These cases show how teaming to innovate can fertilize creativity, clarify goals, and even redefine the meaning of leadership. In these examples, we see products, services, and process innovations that offered valued to companies, customers, or communities. The book synthesizes insights from two decades of research on teams and learning in organizations into a set of actionable recommendations.

Here is an overview and summary of these recommendations:

Aim High

What drives innovation? Let's face it, coming up with and fully developing something new and feasible is hard work. Aim High explains that innovation is best fueled by a compelling purpose that answers the questions, Why care? Why bother? Is it really worth it to focus on doing something new and possibly useful first, and put my ego second? An aspirational and future-oriented goal is very motivating, especially if the link to today's work is clear. This makes it easier to take the risks and suffer the pain of working hard in a demanding environment where nothing is a sure thing. Aiming high also means stretching beyond what seems initially feasible, like rescuing 33 miners trapped under two thousand feet of rock, or bringing six highly visible American hostages out of Iran, or avoiding medical errors in hospitals.

Team Up

Innovation is a team sport. Few worthy aspirations in organizations can be accomplished alone—or even by groups of people who have similar expertise. To produce something new and useful nearly always involves spanning knowledge boundaries. This means team members won't always see eye-to-eye along the way. Although conflict can generate creative new ideas, it can also lead to resentment and frustration and derail innovation. I talk about what it takes to manage differences for the good of the project and how to avoid or mitigate the pitfalls of conflict.

Fail Well

Along the way to achieving worthy aspirations with diverse colleagues, you will almost certainly meet with failures. I explain that the key to failing well is using everyone's experience and insight to think through what we know, in advance, so as to avoid *predictable* failures and to conduct experiments that help fill in knowledge gaps. That way, the failures that do happen will be as smart and as small as possible.

To understand what it means to fail well, we first must clarify three types of failure and then explain why intelligent failures are so vital to innovation. Innovation comes to those who fail often and fail early (because they are finding out what doesn't work). As Thomas Edison said, "Negative results are just what I want. They're just as valuable to me as positive results. I can never find the thing that does the job best until I find the ones that don't."[12]

Learn Fast

Next, I explore what it takes to *learn* from failure, and from other experiences as well. Reflecting together on what happened, what was learned, and what to try next is a crucial step in the innovation process. This has to be done fast and openly, sharing insights widely, so that others in the organization can avoid recreating the same failures a second time. Leaders help this learning process by asking questions that provoke reflection and discussion.

Questions about process and about the causes of failure are particularly valuable. The purpose of reflecting is ultimately to come up with the next experiment, which sometimes means being resigned to pursuing the next failure, followed by more reflection. The secret to organizational learning and innovation is that the learning cycle never stops. The purpose—where the team is headed—usually remains firm; the process—how we do things—can usually be improved.

Repeat

Let's face it. In today's workplace, learning never stops. We achieve some goals and don't achieve others, but the cycle of setting them, finding collaborators, producing intelligent failures, and learning from them keeps on going. Reinforcing this message, I conclude the book with a summary of these recommendations and brief parting thoughts for those leading the innovation journey.

Aim High

Innovation starts with a worthy aspiration. Although invention may occasionally occur as a result of pure brilliance, ingenuity, or the sheer pleasure of discovery, innovation is the result of an effortful and disciplined process. Effort and discipline thrive when people are motivated to strive for something more. Driven by a desire to do something new and useful, people are able and willing to take the risks that innovation entails. So, to foster innovation in your organization, start with some soul searching to identify a worthy aspiration—one that in some small way relates to creating a better world. Whether to create a brand-new product, service, or solution or merely a substantially better way of doing something we already do, innovation begins as a glimmer. An idea. Aiming high for a worthy goal, no matter how distant, engages and motivates people by involving them in something larger than themselves.

Of course, it's possible to innovate without worthy goals or lofty aims, but if you're interested in engaging smart, motivated people in the uncertain journey of innovation, a worthy aspiration is a valuable source of fuel.

In explaining this recommendation, we'll take a look at two dramatic cases of aiming high, along with the innovation journey that ensued: the rescue of the Chilean miners from the San José copper mine in 2010, and the effort to eliminate medical errors at Children's Hospital and Clinics in Minneapolis, Minnesota.

Both cases illustrate innovation through teaming at its best. Each story also highlights the importance of a worthy goal, achieved (not without trepidation, doubt, and even failure) by fluid collaborations among people who contributed their various skills because they believed, often passionately, in that goal.

A Worthy Goal

On August 5, 2010, more than half a million tons of rock collapsed in the San José copper mine in Northern Chile, completely blocking the entrance.[13] Mining accidents are unfortunately common. But this one was unprecedented for several reasons: the distance of the miners from the surface, the sheer number of miners trapped, and the hardness of the rock, to name just a few. Thirty-three men were buried alive, under two thousand feet of rock harder than granite. In Chile, initial estimates of the possibility of finding anyone alive were put at 10 percent— odds that diminished sharply two days later when rescue workers narrowly escaped a secondary collapse of the ventilation shaft, which permanently shut down the option of rescuing the miners through that route.

Yet within 70 days all 33 miners would be rescued. This extraordinary result occurred because several leaders committed to the *aspirational goal of a successful rescue*, despite the brutal odds against their success. That the rescue required innovation is self-evident—there simply was no existing solution, either inside or outside the mining industry, at the outset. It took the collaborative efforts of over one hundred experts in diverse fields innovating to develop and execute a novel solution on the fly.

Innovation occurred in at least two very separate arenas. First, and most painful to consider, were the miners facing the challenge of physical and psychological survival. Innovation here took the form of a new social system—designed to maintain the life and sanity of 33 trapped men in dire circumstances. Second, a network of engineers and geologists came together from multiple organizations and nations to work on the technical problems of locating, reaching, and extracting the trapped miners. Their innovation produced the design and development of a completely novel rescue system. To support the actions of those above and below ground at the San José site, senior leaders in the Chilean government, including the nation's president, made decisions and provided resources and inspiration.

Teaming to Survive

Below ground, amidst shock and fear, leadership and teaming took shape after a tumultuous beginning. Immediately after the collapse, the miners scrambled to safety in the mine's small "refuge."[14] Luis Urzúa, who had formal leadership over the group as the shift supervisor, started by checking provisions in the refuge. Calmly and quickly, he focused on crucial survival needs, especially the limited available food (roughly the amount of food two miners would eat over ten days). However, calm did not prevail. Mario Sepulveda, a charismatic 39-year-old, outraged at the state of the mine and the company's long-standing lack of attention to safety, reacted angrily to the collapse. His energy attracted followers; factions and conflict soon emerged. Some wanted to take action of any kind to reach the outside world rather than sitting helplessly to await rescue. Others wanted to follow Urzúa's guidance. By the end of their first 24 hours, the miners were exhausted by failed attempts to communicate with the outside world and disoriented by the lack of natural light. With scant attention to sanitation or order and subdued by hunger and fatigue, they attempted to sleep.

On the second day, miner José Henríquez stepped in to urge the group to start each day with a collective prayer. Soon this became a sustaining routine and helped unite the group around a shared goal: survival. With no blueprint for how to survive in these conditions, conversation and experimentation were essential to discovering a way forward. In the days that followed, facing darkness, hunger, depression, filth, and illness, the miners cooperated intensely to maintain order, health, sanitation, and sanity.

Teaming to Solve Complex Technical Problems

Above ground, the Chilean Carabineros Special Operations Group—an elite police unit for rescue operations—arrived a few hours after the first collapse. Their initial attempt at rescue led to the ventilation shaft collapse, the rescue effort's dismal first failure. As news of a mine cave-in spread, family members, emergency response teams, rescue workers, and reporters also flooded to the site. Meanwhile, others in the Chilean mining community dispatched experts, drilling machines, and bulldozers. Codelco, the state-owned company overseeing the San José mine, sent Andre Sougarret, an engineer and manager with over 20 years of experience in mining who was known for his composure and ease with people, to lead the operation.

Working with numerous other technical experts, Sougarret formed three teams to oversee different aspects of the operation. One team searched for the men, poking drill holes deep into the earth in the hopes of hearing sounds indicating that the men were alive. Another worked on how to keep them alive if found, and a third worked on how to extract them safely from the refuge.

On October 13, miners began to be brought up, one by one, on a 15-minute journey to the surface. Over the next two days, they were hauled up, one after another, in the 28-inch-wide escape capsule painted with the red, white, and blue of the Chilean flag. After a few minutes to hug relatives, each miner was taken for medical evaluation.

Neither Top-Down nor Bottom-Up

Reflecting on the Chilean rescue, it is clear that a top-down, command-and-control approach—the kind that can be successfully used in a crisis with a known solution, such as when a large fire breaks out or when an impending hurricane is detected—would have failed utterly. No one person, or even one leadership team, could have figured out how to solve this problem. It's also clear that simply encouraging everyone to try anything they wanted would have produced only chaos and harm. Family members, miners, and others with good intentions had to be held back numerous times from rushing headlong at the rock with pickaxes. Instead, what was required, facing the unprecedented scale of the disaster, was coordinated but flexible teaming—multiple temporary groups of people working separately on different types of problems and coordinating across groups, as needed. Such groups innovate in ways no one can anticipate at the outset. Doing this well involves progressive experimentation, a core discipline of innovation.

What should leaders in other enterprises take away from this story? Let's look at two core leadership principles that help drive innovation in any organization.

First, the most senior leadership in the mining disaster committed publicly to a successful outcome, risking both resources and reputation on an unlikely outcome. In his decision to do this, newly elected Chilean president Sebastian Pinera resembles other leaders facing nearly impossible organizational challenges, who have been willing to declare an early and total commitment to the pursuit of success. Aspirational aims are necessarily risky, but they are also motivating.

Second, leaders must demand rapid cycle learning. In this recurring process, everyone must expect and learn from failure. In Chile, technical experts worked together to design, test, modify, and abandon options, over and over again, until they found something that worked. They organized quickly to design and try out various solutions, and equally quickly admitted when these had failed. They willingly changed course based on feedback—some of it obvious (the collapse of the ventilation shaft), some subtle (being told that their measurements were inaccurate by an engineer intruding mid-process with a new technology). Perhaps most importantly, the engineers did not take repeated failure as evidence that a successful rescue was impossible. (Similarly, the miners successfully teamed to solve the most pressing problems of survival, despite the desperate odds.)

Engaging Hearts and Minds

What drives the hard and interpersonally challenging work of teaming for innovation? Let's face it; it's not easy to get up in the morning and come to work knowing you might fail several times before lunch! The hard intellectual and emotional work of innovation is fueled by a compelling purpose that addresses questions like, Why care? Why bother? Why should I put aside the momentary comfort of relaxing in order to exert the effort and subject myself to the risks involved in coming up with new solutions to old problems?

Emotions play a role in generating creative ideas. Emotions spark new connections between disparate experiences. Emotions also motivate and provide a foundation to return to when the going gets tough. The most motivating goals are connected to the objectives and frustrations of *today's* work. This close connection makes tolerable the daily risks and suffering (big and small) in the demanding environment of innovation, where nothing is certain. We can readily see how the emotional pull of saving 33 lives motivated the above-ground innovators in Chile. In other cases, such as the one we'll look at next, the worthy goal is less obvious at the outset. It takes a leader who is passionate about making a difference to point it out.

Leading Innovation at Children's Hospital

Keeping hospitalized patients safe from harm was not widely identified as an important (and surprisingly elusive) goal until the late 1990s. Patient safety is elusive simply because of the complex and variable nature of the work of patient care. Hospitals exemplify the category of complex operations on the Process Knowledge Spectrum, described in this book's introduction.

Hospitals face both obvious and nonobvious challenges. To begin with, some hospitalizations are planned in advance, while others are unpredictable. This makes capacity planning difficult. Second, many different specialists—physicians, pharmacists, nurses, physical therapists, respiratory therapists, and dieticians, to name a few—are involved in the care of each patient, and handoffs from one specialist to another are a major source of risk. Coordinating care among multiple professionals requires extensive communication, which often unfolds in imperfect ways. Each patient is unique, a fact that even the most well-researched protocol cannot change. Third, medical knowledge changes frequently, and many diseases are not well understood. These factors combine to make hospitals far more complex than other high-volume operations, such as assembly lines or call centers. In the face of this complexity, vigilance has long been the de facto strategy for avoiding medical errors. But humans are fallible, and vigilance is an imperfect solution.

In 1999, a leader named Julie Morath set out to do better. To innovate.[15] Her vision? A hospital with 100 percent patient safety. Her solution?

She didn't have one.

Children's Hospital and Clinics in Minneapolis, Minnesota, is a major tertiary care hospital for children, with six facilities located throughout the Minneapolis–St. Paul area. When Morath took the job of chief operating officer at Children's, in 1999, she understood the complexity of patient care operations and clearly recognized the challenge ahead with neither a manual nor a successful predecessor to emulate. To achieve a vision of perfect safety, she would have to invite everyone in the organization to join her in a learning journey. They would have to work together—to team up—to figure out new approaches. Morath thus had a plan, not a solution. The plan included a well-facilitated, well-structured learning journey.

The kind of teaming needed to solve problems in complex organizations such as hospitals involves keen observation from multiple perspectives, timely and open communication, and quick decision making. At Children's, the stakes were high, particularly in the ICU or an operating room, where errors can have dire consequences.

Aiming High with Meaning

Keeping hospitalized children safe: clearly a compelling goal! Importantly, this goal, like most compelling goals, is tied to making a better world. Here, taking interpersonal risks, such as admitting mistakes and pointing out flawed systems to bosses and others, seems worth it. Innovating to improve patient safety gives people an opportunity to make an important positive difference.

When leaders inspire and support teaming for innovation, they are seeking co-investigators, people willing to experiment together to identify and solve problems that have never been solved before. They are embarking on a journey, facing many unknowns.

Morath's goal—to develop an organizational system that never caused avoidable harm to hospitalized children—was articulated at a time when medical errors were rarely discussed among caregivers, let alone by senior management, and were widely considered inevitable by industry insiders because of the complexity noted earlier. Further, knowledge of how to improve safety dramatically was not only limited; it was likely to differ in different parts of the organization, based on the nature of the procedures.

When Morath interviewed for the COO job, she was already talking about patient safety. She had 25 years of patient care administration and had previously been a registered nurse. With her calm demeanor and warm smile, she exuded an unflappable, can-do attitude. At Children's she embarked upon "carefully constructed conversations around the topic of safety with people who would have to be on board with the initiative." In the beginning, this was not easy. As Morath noted, it was "difficult to broach the topic of safety because most people get defensive. Talking about safety implies that we are doing things 'wrong.'"[16]

Soon after assuming her leadership role, Morath assembled a team she called the Patient Safety Steering Committee (PSSC). The PSSC was a select group of key influencers who would help design and launch the "Patient Safety Initiative." To identify those having interest and passion, as well as to communicate with as many people in the hospital as possible, Morath delivered a series of presentations about medical errors, citing the then still unfamiliar fact that as many as 98,000 hospitalized patients in the United States were dying annually from medical errors—more than the number from car accidents, breast cancer, or AIDS. The PSSC was deliberately diverse, comprising doctors and nurses, department heads and frontline staff, union members and executives. It was a group that understood and represented the organization well.

Despite the pedigree of the PSSC and Morath's compelling delivery, many initially pushed back against the idea of a patient safety initiative, reluctant to believe that errors were a problem at Children's. They believed the national statistics but did not believe those numbers applied to Children's. When your work involves taking care of vulnerable children, it's enormously threatening to be told that you might be doing things that harm them. Quite naturally, they resisted Morath's efforts to promote innovation.

Tempting as it must have been to simply reiterate her message more forcefully (given that she understood that all hospitals, because of their operational complexity, were vulnerable to error), Morath did not try to argue the point. Instead, she thoughtfully responded to the resistance with inquiry. "Okay, this data may not be applicable here," she concurred. Then she probed gently, "Tell me, what was your own experience this week, in the units, with your patients? Was everything as safe as you would like it to have been?"[17]

The Power of Inquiry

This simple inquiry seems to have transformed the dialogue. Note its features. Her question is an invitation, one that is genuine, curious, direct, and concrete. Each caregiver is invited to consider his or her own patients and experiences, in his or her own unit, over the prior few days. Moreover, the question is aspirational—not, "Did you see things that were unsafe?" but rather, "Was everything as safe as you would like it to have been?" It respects others' experience while it invites aspiration.

Too many would-be leaders forget about the power of inquiry and instead rely on forceful advocacy to bring others along. As Morath showed, inquiry respects and invites. As people began to discuss with her and with others incidents they had thought were unique or idiosyncratic, they realized that most of their colleagues had experienced similar events. As Morath put it, "I found that most people had been at the center of a health care situation where something did not go well. They were quick to recognize that the hospital could be doing better." She led as many as 18 focus groups throughout the organization to allow people to air their concerns and ideas.

Making It Safe to Talk About Problems

To build the psychological safety needed for the inevitably difficult conversations about errors and failures, Morath frequently described her philosophy on patient safety—to anyone who would listen. In her words, "Health care is a very complex system, and complex systems are, by their very nature, risk-prone. The culture of health care must be one of everyone working together to understand safety, identify risks, and report them without fear of blame. We must look at ways to change the whole system when we manage to zero defects." By emphasizing the systemic nature of failures, she sought to help people move away from a tendency to find and blame individual culprits.

Morath knew firsthand about the aftershock and emotional pain of medical accidents for healthcare workers. She never forgot one she'd witnessed 30 years earlier, when she was a young nurse: a four-year-old patient died from an anesthesia error. What Morath remembered, even more than the devastation of the child's death, was that "the nurse who felt responsible 'went home that day and never returned,' giving up the career she loved due to a profound and crushing feeling of guilt. Doctors and other nurses 'just shut down' and never talked to one another about what happened. The hospital's attorneys swooped in to do damage control. 'It just didn't sit right and it plagued me,' Morath said decades later."

So she introduced a new system for reporting medical incidents called "blameless reporting." The idea was to allow people to communicate confidentially or anonymously about medical accidents without being punished for doing so, so as to bring as many of these problems as possible to light, to determine their underlying causes, and to keep caring professionals in their positions.

Morath also instituted new words—new ways of talking about safety lapses that would be less emotionally threatening. For example, she encouraged people to substitute "study" for "investigation." To Morath, study meant a way of learning how systems work and how the pieces fit together. An investigation, on the other hand, was more like a police lineup, assigning blame to someone in a linear search to determine a single cause. By avoiding words that implied blame and encouraging language conducive to learning from failures, Morath was trying to make it psychologically safe to talk about error.

Just as important, she believed that the whole meaning of "error" had to be reframed. She explained to people that in hospitals, "accidents" (a term preferable to "error") arose from faulty systems rather than faulty persons. Complex systems are failure-prone; individual clinicians involved in a system failure are victims of that complexity, just like their patients.

Lastly, "blame" was to be replaced by the word "accountable," defined as being responsible for the duties of a particular job and whatever knowledge it required, as well as for understanding the larger system in which one was a human component. All of these linguistic interventions were designed to make it safe to engage in the interpersonally risky behaviors of innovation.

When leaders successfully engage employees in an innovation process, ideas start to bubble up, experiments start to happen, and activities start to take hold and spread. To a manager seeking to "get the job done," the process might at first seem laborious and slow. But engaging people as active thinkers and learners is the only way to innovate in a complex system like a hospital, where solutions simply don't exist at the outset.

It's a Stretch

On the innovation journey, aiming high means stretching beyond what seems initially feasible. The aspiration must be truly challenging. At the same time, it's important that it not be completely implausible. The distinction can be a very fine line. The goal should inspire but not turn off or depress those who wish to innovate. Developing systems whereby patients are safe from medical mishap is one such goal. It's enormously challenging, but through innovative ways of changing the culture of reporting and by introducing better mechanisms for catching and correcting small process failures before they reach patients, it is not impossible to dramatically improve patient safety. Morath's innovation journey was both cultural and procedural.

Another example in the same industry comes from the recent innovation called "accountable care organizations," or ACOs. The concept is basically that healthcare delivery organizations agree to be paid a monthly fixed amount, in advance, for providing care to a set of patients—in contrast to the traditional fee-for-service approach. For many, the ACO model, which rewards organizations that reduce healthcare costs and raise quality performance at the same time, is one of the most promising innovations in healthcare.

Richard J. Gilfillan, MD, joined the "Innovation Center" of the U.S. government's Centers for Medicare and Medicaid Services (CMS) in 2010 to lead the change that would manifest new value-based payment initiatives, including ACOs. Soon after joining CMS, he articulated three simple, clear goals: better care, better health, and dramatically lower costs. His stretch goal? Saving Medicare $1.1 billion by 2016.[18]

Much like Morath at Children's, Gilfillan recognized the need for large-scale system changes early in his tenure. He quickly assembled a team of 73 unpaid private sector "innovation advisers" to act as go-betweens for project administrators and his team at CMS. He understood the scale of the networks involved and the heavy lifting required. "There's no shortage of innovation in healthcare," he told a group at a Healthcare Innovation Summit in June 2011, "but we don't have a business model that rewards innovation." "We are looking," he said, for organizations willing to "shift their business models."[19]

Gilfillan's strategy was to recruit a small group of brave healthcare delivery leaders willing to participate in a pilot of the ACO "Advanced Payment" model. Some of these would lead critical care urban hospitals, and others led low-volume rural hospitals; both would agree to receive advance monthly payments instead of fees for individual visits and procedures. Reaching out, he found people like Susan Thompson, president and CEO of Iowa-based Trinity Health Systems (with their partner, the Trimark Physicians Group), willing to innovate in the risky pilot. Trinity delivers health services within an eight-county service area in central Iowa.[20] This huge network meant that Thompson had an opportunity to effectively coordinate the care of her region's patients. But to get everyone on board with the plan, she needed everyone to help her innovate. As we will see in "Team Up," her own high aspiration to make a difference is starting to pay off.

Worthy Aspirations That Motivate Innovation

The opportunity to make a difference turns out to be a key driver of innovation. When people share an ambitious goal—together with a vision of a better future—it gives them a shared identity. It builds camaraderie.

What's so great about camaraderie? First, it makes work more fun. Second, people feel safer, and when people feel safer it's easier to be creative. And third, because innovation is heavy lifting, people must have confidence in each other's abilities. Envisioning a process or a product that has never existed requires conviction. For this reason, the goal, as noted, should be a stretch, but not absurd!

Finally, as any reader who has experienced true teamwork in the pursuit of innovation knows well, there's nothing better. At times, you believe that anything's possible when a group of dedicated people put their minds to doing what was thought to be impossible.

Innovation is a team sport. But teaming to innovate isn't always a smooth ride. Next, I explain why people must span boundaries, build psychological safety, and cool conflict to make teaming work and allow innovation to flourish.

Team Up

Like it or not, innovation is a team sport. Few worthy innovations are accomplished alone or even by groups of people who have the same basic knowledge and expertise. Here we look at what it takes to team and explain why teaming is more challenging than it might first appear. We explore the crucial role of psychological safety—along with other enabling factors—in helping people team effectively. And because teaming across disciplinary lines is so vital to innovation, we'll pay particular attention to the types of boundaries people confront when teaming to innovate, and how to bridge them effectively. We'll start with a story that showcases just about every kind of seemingly insurmountable boundary imaginable.

Strange Bedfellows

It is hard to imagine two more different thought-worlds than Hollywood and the CIA. But what makes the story of the fate of six American hostages in Iran truly gripping is the teaming between these strange bedfellows, and how it brought the hostages home. As you read this story, consider the types of boundaries between these players, the nature of the teaming that occurred, and the innovative solution itself. How did teaming up across boundaries produce innovation?

Early in the morning of November 4, 1979, at the United States Embassy in Tehran, Iran's capital city, a rapidly growing crowd of anti-American student protestors was demanding that ousted monarch ("Shah") Mohammad Reza Pahlavi be returned from U.S. exile. They wanted him to be tried by the revolutionary government led by Ayatollah Khomeini. The crowd rushed the embassy gates, chanting, "*Allahu Akbar!*" (God is great!) and "*Marg bar Amrika!*" (Death to America!). Soon students were scaling the walls of the embassy. Within minutes, the protestors swarmed the vast compound that contained the ambassador's residence and staff offices.[21]

Consular diplomat Martin Lijek, in Iran on his first consular post, hoped the adjacent visa-processing building where he worked would not be in the protestors' path. He hoped that no one would suspect that a small collection of American embassy staff, Iranian employees, and visa applicants was on the second floor.[22] Martin's group included his wife, Cora (consular assistant), Joseph Stafford (senior foreign service officer), Stafford's wife, Kathleen (consular assistant), and Robert Anders (senior consular officer).

Suddenly, the building went dark as power was cut. Gunshots rang out in the compound. Escaping capture was paramount: Iranian employees had known neighbors who were apprehended and executed by revolutionary guards. As the crowd neared their building, Martin and his peers destroyed the plates used to make visa stamps, improvised an evacuation plan, and ushered both staff and applicants to the back door. This was the sole exit on the embassy compound with direct street access.

The Iranian visa applicants exited first, in small groups, ahead of the American staff. One Iranian group was captured moments later and taken back to the embassy. The Lijeks, Staffords, and Anders headed to the British Embassy, several blocks away. The American escapees had almost reached the embassy when they encountered another demonstration.

Eventually, the group found refuge in the residence of Ken Taylor, the Canadian ambassador. The six became known at the State Department and CIA as the "houseguests." Aware that the lives of the Canadian ambassador and his so-called houseguests were at risk if the presence of the Americans became known, experts in Washington, D.C., were considering a number of rescue plans, mostly involving overland routes bypassing roads and checkpoints.

Tony Mendez, Graphics Authentication Division head at the CIA, was called in to come up with a plan for bringing the hostages home. False identities were Mendez's specialty. He had spent 14 years in the CIA's Office of Technical Service—a real-world version of James Bond's "Q" branch—and had helped more than a hundred agents and others escape life-threatening situations abroad.

The problem was that neither the Canadian nor American diplomatic corps leaders could conceive of a credible reason for any North Americans to be in Tehran after the hostage crisis had begun. Teachers, agricultural researchers, and others had all left. In the midst of the brainstorming, Mendez had a unique idea: to assemble a film scouting crew.

The plan was fleshed out as follows. Mendez would play the role of fictitious film producer "Kevin Harkins" from Canada, and request a "location scout" trip to Iran for a Hollywood studio film. The concept seemed plausible because so-called Hollywood creative types might conceivably be oblivious to the situation in revolutionary Iran. Focusing on finding the right backdrop for a new movie, perhaps a science fiction story in need of an exotic desert landscape, a Hollywood producer might just be crazy enough to scout out the view in Iran. Moreover, the Iranian government wanted the hard currency and might welcome this kind of business venture. A film production could mean millions of U.S. dollars.

Pursuing this idea, Mendez needed partners. The cover story seemed plausible. But a great deal of work still needed to be done to fill in the details for an operation that could withstand scrutiny while manhunting Americans was in high gear. To prepare the foundation for this cover, Mendez flew to Los Angeles in mid-January to meet John Chambers, a veteran makeup artist who had won a 1969 Academy Award for *Planet of the Apes* and was also a longtime Mendez collaborator. Chambers invited makeup artist and special effects expert Bob Sidell to join the meeting.

Mendez, Chambers, and Sidell brainstormed to figure out and then execute all of the details to create a fake Hollywood production company. They rented space, designed business cards, and concocted detailed identities for each of the six members of the location-scouting team, including their former film credits. The production company secured a suite at Sunset Gower Studios.

Chambers found a well-suited script in the vast archives of submitted screenplays never filmed. Mendez gave the script a new title, *Argo*, the name of the vessel used by Greek mythology hero Jason (and his Argonauts) on his daring voyage across the world to retrieve the Golden Fleece. Mendez and Chambers designed a full-page ad for the film to run in key trade magazines *Variety* and the *Hollywood Reporter.* As additional "pocket litter" to boost his Hollywood credentials, Mendez collected matchbooks from the famous Brown Derby restaurant in Beverly Hills, where the production crew gathered the evening before his departure for Iran.

Finally, Mendez obtained false Canadian passports for the six and flew to Tehran. Meeting the hostages, he explained the cover story and presented Jack Kirby's conceptual art, the screenplay, the ad in *Variety*, and the "Studio Six" business cards. With some reluctance, the houseguests agreed the ruse could work and set about memorizing their new identities to match their fake Canadian passports. Soon they were headed to the Tehran airport to make their dangerous escape from Iran—in plain sight.

After several tense moments at the gate, Mendez and his "film crew" boarded the plane. The plane took off, and Mendez and the six escapees breathed a collective sigh of relief. Together they had successfully accomplished the most creative and improbable "exfiltration" of Mendez's career.

Teaming Across Boundaries

Mendez, the houseguests, the Canadians who sheltered them, and the creative artists in Hollywood who made it all believable had little in common. They came from different backgrounds, different organizations, different areas of expertise, and different cultures. Yet they collaborated to execute a remarkable and remarkably innovative operation. This kind of diversity involves boundaries between people from different identity groups.

What's in a Boundary?

Think of the adjectives you might use to describe yourself. Some of these adjectives describe identity groups, such as gender, occupation, or nationality. Some identity groups, and their corresponding boundaries, are more visible than others. Gender, for example, is visible. Occupation is less visible, except where clothing gives it away.

What is invisible, however, are the *taken-for-granted assumptions*, or mind-sets, that people in different groups hold. For teaming to be successful, people must be aware that they come together with different perspectives, almost always taking for granted the "rightness" of their own beliefs and values. It's not enough to simply say, "Let's band together," and it will all work out. No matter how much goodwill is involved and how important the goal is, boundaries limit collaboration in ways that are both invisible and powerful.[23]

Education (level and type), along with the socializing processes that occur when we interact with others in our field, contributes to unconscious beliefs that the knowledge shared by one's own group is especially important. It's as if a wall separates engineers from marketers, nurses from doctors, and designers in Beijing from designers in Boston. The knowledge and skills we learn in a given field of expertise make up the visible curriculum. The invisible curriculum teaches us to forget what it was like not to know what we know.

The most important thing to understand about boundaries, then, is that most people take the knowledge that lies on *their* side of a boundary for granted. This can make it hard to communicate with those on the other side. But at its core, teaming is about reaching across or spanning such boundaries. To do this, we must first be keenly aware of what they are and what they do.

Taken-for-granted assumptions are, by definition, hard to recognize. The first step in doing so is becoming aware that they exist, so you can be on the lookout for them. Consider the example of two aeronautical businesses that joined forces to work on an innovative new aircraft.[24] At the first planning meeting, everyone agreed on ambitious goals and a demanding schedule. Despite this agreement, the conversation kept getting mired in misunderstanding and miscommunication. Finally, it was discovered that the two groups meant something different when they used the simple phrase, "the plane has been delivered." One organization understood it to mean the plane has been physically delivered to a control station. The other understood the exact same phrase to mean the plane has been delivered to the physical site and the machinery has passed all technical inspection. This semantic difference was crucial to the project because it affected how data were to be collected and categorized. This subtle difference between two groups is just a single example of the kind of misunderstanding that can be multiplied many times over when teaming spans boundaries.

Types of Boundaries

Three types of boundaries are particularly important in the context of teaming to innovate: physical distance (location, time zone, and so on), status (perceived social value, hierarchical level, profession, and so on), and knowledge (experience, education, and so on).[25]

Physical distance. In many companies, work teams in globally dispersed locations—so-called virtual teams—are used to integrate expertise. They're virtual because they work together using communication technologies like email, phone, or Skype. The potential for innovation from such teaming is great; however, the challenges are equally so. Without face-to-face contact, taken-for-granted assumptions can be particularly tricky to recognize and address.

Status. The most common status differences at work are profession-based status and level in the organizational hierarchy. Professional status particularly influences speaking-up behavior. In healthcare, for example, physicians have more status and power than nurses, who in turn have more status than technicians. Yet members across these professions almost always have to team up to take care of patients. So patients are at risk if people don't learn how to team across status boundaries. This is what Susan Thompson at Trinity Health Systems realized when she launched one of the earliest accountable care organizations in the United States (as noted in "Aim High"). Thompson asked primary care physicians, specialists, nurses, and other clinicians to team up across status lines to coordinate care in order to improve patient outcomes and at the same time reduce the cost of care. The only thing that surprised her? How quickly the innovation produced results: "In just 11 months, overall inpatient hospital utilization has declined 25 percent, 30-day readmissions have declined 43 percent, frequent emergency department patients are now receiving more consistent care and patient satisfaction scores have improved."[26]

Knowledge. Teaming to innovate is most often about bridging across areas of expertise. In product and process development teams, in particular, bringing together people from different organizational functions for a limited period of intense teaming is increasingly common.

In product development, engineering offers insight into design and technology; manufacturing, into feasible production processes, accurate cost estimates, and pilot and full-scale production; and marketing, into customer receptivity, customer segments, product positioning, and product plans. Combining these diverse skill sets and perspectives is as crucial as it is challenging, because misunderstandings arise due to different meanings embedded in different disciplines, and mistrust often follows.

Organization and occupation are both important sources of knowledge boundaries. Organizational boundaries exist anytime people from different companies—or even sites within a company—have to work together. Occupational boundaries come from the training or education through which experts gain mastery over a specialized body of knowledge. This gives them a particular mind-set, a way of knowing. And that mastery becomes taken for granted. The jargon acquired in specialized education and practice constitutes a kind of foreign language for others. This makes working together—across the "thought-worlds" of occupational communities—vulnerable to misunderstanding.

Meanwhile, in most fields specialization is intensifying. The rate of new knowledge development requires people to invest considerable time just to stay current. This of course makes it even harder to master other disciplines. In technical fields the explosion of new knowledge makes narrow specialization especially likely. Fields spawn new subfields, and they in turn spawn even more specialized subfields. For example, electrical engineering, once a subfield of physics, became its own discipline by 1900, and today it splits into distinct subfields like power systems, signal processing, and computer architecture. When an area of specialization is narrow, it's unlikely that practical innovations that benefit ordinary people will occur there without combining different specializations together. Innovation requires teaming across knowledge boundaries. Whether developing a new cell phone or discovering a cure for diabetes, it is essential to find novelty and synergy from the unexpected combinations of ideas and techniques that can occur between fields of expertise.

What It Takes to Team

The time pressures we all experience today mean that a highly structured approach, in which managers plan each aspect of a large innovation project, dividing it into specialized tasks to be accomplished separately in phases, is unrealistic. Such planning becomes even less realistic when completed tasks are "thrown over the wall" to other functions or disciplines, because those on the other side of the wall are unlikely to fully understand what they're receiving. Instead, the walls between disciplines have to come down, and simultaneous work on related tasks must be coordinated and negotiated on a dynamic teaming journey.

The strikingly innovative (visually and functionally) aquatics center built for the 2008 Beijing Olympics and dubbed the "Water Cube" is a particularly good example of the innovation that can come from cross-boundary teaming—when it works!

At the outset, the goal was both clear and motivating, exemplifying the maxim *Aim high*: Build a memorable, iconic building for swimming and diving that would reflect Chinese culture, integrate with the site, and minimize energy consumption. It had to be aesthetically striking, "green," unprecedented, and on time. It also had to involve both Chinese and Western traditions in order to appeal to the selection committee and to millions of spectators. Moving from concept to completion in record time, the Water Cube utilized cross-disciplinary, cross-continental, and cross-organizational teaming. Led by Tristram Carfrae, principal and senior structural engineer at Arup in Sydney, Australia, the teaming involved more than 80 individuals from four organizations (Arup, PTW Architects, China State Construction and Engineering Company, and China Construction Design International). They were spread across 20 disciplines in four countries.[27]

In the process, diverse experts came together at several points to talk about design ideas and to brainstorm possibilities—rather than just getting quickly to work on a single design. In these conversations, they explicitly dug into how the cultural meanings of design elements might differ across nations. Interacting across different cultures was a significant challenge. One technique that worked well was exchanging specialists who had familiarity with both cultures, asking them to go work in the other firm for a period. These literal boundary-spanners helped project members to get interested in each other's language, norms, practices, and expectations. The result, as we've all seen, was a magnificent 340,000-square-foot building framed in steel and covered with semitransparent, eco-efficient blue bubbles, housing 17,000 spectators—and winning numerous prestigious engineering and design awards.

Nowadays, it's just not possible for individuals, no matter how expert, to develop important innovations all by themselves. The chances of individual parts, developed separately, coming together into meaningful, functional wholes—a new product, feature film, or rescue operation—without intense communication across boundaries are exceedingly low. How can the boundaries between diverse groups be overcome? Curiosity, psychological safety, and process guidelines are three of the key ingredients.

Mutual Curiosity

Genuine curiosity about what others think, worry about, and aspire to achieve is invaluable for crossing boundaries. By cultivating our own curiosity about what makes others tick, each of us can contribute to creating an environment where it's acceptable to express interest in others' thoughts and feelings. MIT professor Ed Schein, a preeminent researcher on corporate culture, uses the term "temporary cultural island" in his description of a process for sharing crucial professional and personal information in a multicultural work group. (Note that the term "culture" applies to nations, companies, professions, and other identity groups.) The process involves talking about concrete experiences and feelings, and is fueled by thoughtful questions on the part of a leader acting as a facilitator. Schein explains that cultural assumptions related to authority and intimacy are crucial issues in culturally diverse teams. When someone in one culture violates an authority rule that is taken for granted in another culture, for example by speaking in an overly familiar manner to a high-status person, someone may experience the behavior as jarring. When we share stories in which these issues are exposed, boundaries begin to dissolve.[28]

Psychological Safety

Boundaries will not be spanned and innovation cannot flourish in an environment that lacks psychological safety. Psychological safety describes an interpersonal climate where people feel able to express ideas, ask questions, quickly acknowledge mistakes, and raise concerns about the project early and often. They also feel responsible for doing so. It's not that it's *easy* for them to take these interpersonal risks; rather, they understand it's expected of them. It is part of collaboration. They recognize too that teaming up is as interpersonally challenging as it is rewarding. Without these behaviors—which can feel especially risky in hierarchies—successful innovation is unlikely. Table 2 depicts leadership actions that help build a climate of psychological safety where innovation can thrive.

In fast-paced, cross-disciplinary, cross-border teaming, as in the Water Cube project, it's not easy for people to quickly share their ideas and expertise. Some people worry about what others will think of them. Some fear that they will be less valuable if they give away what they know. Others are reluctant to show off. Even accepting others' ideas can be difficult if it feels like an admission of weakness. Because vital interpersonal exchanges don't always happen spontaneously, leaders must facilitate them. A basic approach to creating psychological safety as a leader is to model the behaviors on which teaming depends, such as asking thoughtful questions or acknowledging your own ignorance about a topic or area of expertise. Leaders who act this way make it safer for everyone else to do it too. Understanding this, engineering team leader Carfrae created what Water Cube team members referred to as a "safe design environment."

Process Guidelines

In any complex teaming effort it is important to establish process guidelines that everyone agrees to follow. A

Table 2. Leadership Behaviors That Build Psychological Safety

Behavior	Description
Be accessible	Leaders encourage team members to learn together by being accessible and personally involved.
Acknowledge limits	When leaders admit that they don't know something, their genuine display of humility encourages other team members to follow suit.
Display fallibility	To create psychological safety, team leaders must demonstrate a tolerance of failure by acknowledging their own fallibility.
Invite participation	When people believe their leaders value their input, they're more engaged and responsive.
Frame failures as learning opportunities	Instead of punishing people for well-intentioned risks that backfire, leaders encourage team members to embrace error and deal with failure in a productive manner.
Use direct language	Using direct, actionable language instigates the type of straightforward, blunt discussion that enables learning.
Set boundaries	When leaders are as clear as possible about what is acceptable, people feel psychologically safer than when boundaries are vague or unpredictable.

strategy for boundary management is essential. Guidelines are needed for specifying points at which separate teaming activities must come together to coordinate resources and decisions. Carfrae and his team thus adopted a strategy for "interface management" that divided the project into "volumes" based on physical and temporal boundaries. Each volume was owned by a subteam. An interface existed when anything touched or crossed a boundary. Regular interface coordination meetings were held to manage physical, functional, contractual, and operational boundaries. Through extensive documentation, the team eliminated mistakes that might otherwise have occurred at these boundaries—saving materials and funds, and sparing headaches.

When Conflict Heats Up

Even when psychological safety, curiosity, and process guidelines are in place, the very nature of teaming is such that conflict will occur. In fact, conflict is desirable. Without conflict—the competing ideas from which new possibilities sometimes spring—innovation is less likely. But however appealing the idea of creative conflict is in theory, in practice managing conflict effectively is hard to do.

The trouble is, when we encounter differences of opinion, especially those based on values or beliefs we hold deeply, it can trigger strong emotions. Emotions can hijack reason, temporarily of course, making it hard to sift through the differences and find the important questions, ideas, and new possibilities that may be lurking. It takes skill to cool one's own and others' emotions so as to put conflict to good use.[29]

What set of skills is necessary to transform hot tensions into creativity and innovation? It starts with understanding the difference between hot and cool cognition.

Hot and Cool Cognition

Research by cognitive psychologists Janet Metcalfe and Walter Mischel showed that we each have two distinct cognitive systems through which we process events, which they called hot and cool.[30] The hot system, when engaged, triggers people to respond emotionally and quickly. In this case they are often said to speak or act in the heat of the moment. The cool system, in contrast, is deliberate and careful. When using our cool system, we can slow down and gather our thoughts. The cool system is the basis for self-regulation and self-control.

It is desperately needed to team effectively in the face of conflict.

Think about the last time you found yourself debating an important issue at work, especially one you really cared about. Many such conversations go back and forth, with people repeating the same points over and over again. Conflicts heat up when people hold different values or belief systems, or have different interests and incentives. This can make it hard to process the conflict productively, and hard to find the seeds of something new and innovative.

In a company I'll refer to as Elite Manufacturing (to protect its confidentiality), I studied eight senior managers over several months as they met to design a new corporate strategy. I observed as two senior executives got embroiled in a conflict that quickly turned personal—merely because each man took for granted that his own perspective was right, and to him obviously so. To each, the other's disagreement seemed deliberately obstructive.

One executive believed the future of the industry lay in low-end, inexpensive products, and he said so. The other argued that the way to have a significant advantage was to offer distinctive, high-design products that stood out in a sea of cheap alternatives. Already the conflict was heating up.

As often happens in the face of uncertainty, conflicting interpretations of the same facts were used to fuel conflicting truths in the strategy debate. Such conflicts quickly reach an impasse, and the discussion gets personal. It's hard for people not to see each other's viewpoint as wrongheaded, and deliberately so. Each sees the other as stubborn or, worse, manipulative. They fall victim to what's called the fundamental attribution error. And whether blaming each other's motives, character, or abilities, people in the midst of a tough conflict usually silently blame someone else for the lack of progress on the issues. Although very human, this spontaneous reasoning severely hampers innovation.

Three Practices That Cool Hot Conflict

The key question is this: How can people effectively use different perspectives to produce innovation rather than unproductive conflict? The answer lies in understanding how to cool hot topics in fast-paced conversations at work.

To cool conflict down and find effective ways to build on others' ideas and perspectives, my colleague

Diana Smith and I recommend three practices.[31] We refer to them as managing self, managing conversations, and managing relationships. Although these practices are not easy, with practice it's possible to become skilled in their use.

Managing self. This practice involves recognizing one's emotions for what they are: spontaneous personal reactions to a situation. Emotions let us know that we care about the discussion at hand, and we need to slow ourselves down to pay very close attention to what's happening. Managing self means learning how to quickly reflect—to turn our curiosity inward for a brief period and ask ourselves *why* we're feeling anxious, or frustrated, or angry. It's critical to remind oneself in these situations of two essential facts. First is the very real likelihood that you are missing part of the picture (the part that others see!). Second is that you too are contributing to the problem—in the same way you're convinced the other person is doing so.

Managing conversations. This practice starts with realizing that conversations don't manage themselves. It takes a bit of guidance for a conversation that has crossed knowledge boundaries and run into conflicting perspectives to go well and produce good results. To facilitate good communication in the face of heated conflict, it's necessary to slow the conversation down so as to combine thoughtful statements with thoughtful questions. This allows people to understand the true basis of a disagreement and to identify the rationale behind different positions. Doing this well also means inviting quiet voices into the discussion, to bring new perspectives and new facts to light.

Managing relationships. While the first two practices are skills that are needed in the heat of a disagreement, the third is the ongoing practice of building strong relationships that can withstand the temporary assault of disagreement. Managers who take the time to get to know each other as people and to understand the other's goals and concerns are less likely to attribute selfish motives to each other and more likely to be curious about others' concerns. Managing relationships is about building trust grounded in experience. Investing time in getting to know colleagues—new and old—helps lay the foundation for productive conflict, despite the emotions that will surely surface along the way.

All three practices were used at Elite to defuse the conflict and figure out how to innovate the 50-year-old company's strategy. By sharing the personal experiences and deeper rationales behind their positions, members of the strategy team began to build respect and trust. Each executive started to become curious about what motivated the others' positions. As this happened, one executive, who had not spoken up previously, pointed out that Elite was in tricky territory that differed in fundamental ways from the challenges faced in the past. Another suggested listing crucial topics: How will we compete? How will we reduce costs? Do we need to redefine Elite's core mission?

By slowing down to figure out what really lay behind their differing positions, these senior managers learned how to reflect on and challenge their own spontaneous emotional reactions. They became willing to experiment with reframing a situation, or looking at it from a different perspective. Reflecting and reframing are essential skills for cooling a hot conflict. They can interrupt emotional hijackings before they erupt and bring a team's progress to a halt.

It's not possible to manage conflict by simply avoiding emotions. Our emotions are spontaneous and natural. To suggest we avoid them in difficult conversations is a fool's errand. Instead, we have to learn how to be thoughtful and open about them. We have to be willing to dig a little more deeply into what they are telling us. This is essential because innovation almost always involves the effective use of differences. Learning how to talk about what makes us tick and what lies underneath our opinions helps to build the genuine, resilient relationships that are crucial to effective teaming. Once the Elite executives realized that none of them had the corner on truth, they were willing to temporarily put aside ideological and personal differences to think about a new range of issues with their colleagues.

Embracing the Risks of Teaming

Innovation involves people. And people, as we all know, are complicated creatures.

Because innovation requires problem solving on so many levels, from practical skills to expertise and creativity, teaming to innovate often involves a great deal of diversity. In fact, the greater the diversity among team members—in backgrounds, skills, and expertise—the greater the likelihood of success, but also the greater the likelihood of misunderstandings and problematic conflict. The teaming practices described above can help innovation teams overcome these very real challenges to success.

We've just covered some of the important challenges to teaming for innovation, but one of the biggest (the elephant in the room) looms ahead: *failure*. Failing often and well is a critical piece of the innovation process. Failing well, as we will explore next, is all about making sense of what we know and don't know, and figuring out what to try next.

Let's take a look.

Fail Well

Every child learns at some point that failure is bad and dodging blame is a winning strategy. By the time we're working adults, avoiding association with failure is all but second nature. This self-protective reflex may keep our reputation intact (or at least most people seem to think it does), but it harms the companies we work for. Why? It is nearly impossible to learn from failures if people don't admit and analyze them. In any industry where innovation is crucial for survival, an ability to learn from failure is an essential skill.

Learning from failure thus begins with unlearning. This is because childish notions of success are intimately twined with self-esteem, status, and the need for approval. As adults we understand that knowledge is in constant flux, technology insists on changing fast, and confronting new and unfamiliar situations is simply part of working in the 21st century. Expecting failure-free performance is illogical in this dynamic context. Moreover, if we want to innovate, we have to unlearn spontaneous responses about failure. We have to reprogram. Unlearning the idea that failure is bad starts with a deeper understanding of failure.

Unpacking Failure

Over the last 20 years of research and consulting within organizations in a variety of industries, I've seen managers really struggle to embrace the reality that failure is an essential prerequisite to innovation. In fact, the exhortation to *fail well* sounds to them like a nonsensical oxymoron. This is because they haven't fully recognized that failures come in several different types, not all (in fact, few) of them blameworthy.

I will describe three basic types of failure: *preventable, complex,* and *intelligent.*[32] I'll also talk about how to design intelligent failures and how to be courageous. Avoiding preventable failures is both important and feasible. Complex failures can be hard to predict, but with vigilance they too can be largely avoided. In contrast, intelligent failures are in fact positive events. They're part of an essential strategy for creating new knowledge, developing ideas, and producing innovation. Failing well means engaging in intelligent failures. It also means learning quickly when complex failures occur, or nearly occur, so as to avoid any future recurrence. A primary aspect of failing well is avoiding the "blame game" so that you can use failure to promote innovation.

Many leaders worry that in the absence of blame there's no accountability, and without accountability employees won't work hard. The truth is, a culture that makes it safe to be honest, safe to report failure, and safe to admit mistakes is a culture in which a responsible adult can thrive and do his or her best work. Why? Because most people want to feel proud of the work they do, to be part of something larger than themselves, and to make a difference in the lives of colleagues and customers. Given the right conditions, they will. To understand this better, consider that the reasons for failure, as described in the next section and illustrated in Table 3, fall along a spectrum from blameworthy to praiseworthy. Yes, you read that right. Praiseworthy!

Failure's Causes

Let's start with the obvious cause. *Deliberate violation*, in which a person chooses to violate a prescribed procedure or rule, clearly anchors the blameworthy end of the spectrum. *Inattention*, in which someone inadvertently deviates from what's required because he or she lost focus or got distracted—well, that's a little less clear. Inattention could be due to texting when you should be looking at the road. That's blameworthy. Or it could occur when a worker is put in the problematic situation of working a double shift, and fatigue has made perfect attentiveness impossible. There's blame involved here, but it belongs to the manager who put the worker in that situation, not to the worker himself. Next on my spectrum is *lack of competence*. This describes a situation in which an individual doesn't have or hasn't been taught the necessary skills to do the job (hmmm, whose fault is that?).

Inadequate process describes a situation in which an individual, or a group, faces a faulty or incomplete set of guidelines. This often occurs when a process is new and the kinks haven't been worked out yet. *Task challenge* describes situations in which the task at hand is simply too difficult to be successfully executed every time. For a simple illustration, consider the elite figure skater able to perform the extraordinary feat of a quadruple Lutz to embellish a winning Olympic routine. Given that no skater pulled off this extremely difficult move in a competition until 2011, it's clear that the quadruple Lutz is too challenging to support a realistic expectation that any skater can do it perfectly every time. When a failure to execute an exceedingly challenging task occurs, it would be just plain wrong to call that blameworthy.

Next, some situations are exceedingly complex. When Hurricane Sandy hit New York City in the fall of 2012, responding successfully meant bringing an enormous number of different people and actions to bear on a fast-moving problem with many affected people, buildings, and organizations. Even though good protocols were in place for hurricane response, *complexity* means that it was unlikely that everything would work perfectly—that is, that no failures (small or large) would occur along the way. New York's emergency response system performed admirably, but this didn't mean that nothing went wrong and no one got hurt.

Relatedly, *uncertainty* means we don't have complete knowledge about future events. Given what they know at the time, people will take reasonable actions that nonetheless may produce undesirable results (failures). Note that it would be unreasonable to blame anyone for such failures; the appropriate reaction would be something like, "We did the best we could with the knowledge we had."

Finally, some failures happen as a result of experimentation. Consider two kinds of experiments. First, *hypothesis-testing experiments* test a specific prediction. They might be focused on whether a new packaging design will appeal to customers, for example. Sometimes our hypotheses are right. Sometimes they are wrong (failure again!). Either way, we've learned something. It's better to find out that customers don't like the packaging before we roll it out at full scale. *Exploratory experiments*, in contrast to experiments driven by a focused hypothesis, are conducted to investigate a possibility, without a strong sense of what we expect to happen. They expand our knowledge of some area through exploratory action.

Considering the range of causes along this spectrum, it should be clear that deliberate violation is the only action for which a person obviously deserves to be blamed. After that, from inattention all the way through to exploratory experiments, it would be harder to come to that conclusion. This would require us to ignore the effects of fatigue, poor training, poor management, or novelty (see Table 3). In fact, any failure resulting from honest effort or thoughtful experimentation is grist for the innovation mill and thus should instead be considered praiseworthy.

Table 3. A Spectrum of Potential Causes of Organizational Failures[33]

Potential Cause of Failure	Description	Is Blame Appropriate?
Deliberate violation	An individual chooses to violate a prescribed process or practice.	Yes
Inattention	An individual inadvertently deviates from a prescribed process or practice.	Maybe
Lack of ability	An individual doesn't have the skills, conditions, or training to execute a job.	Unlikely
Inadequate process	An individual adheres to a prescribed process, but the process is faulty or incomplete.	Unlikely
Task challenge	An individual faces a task that is too difficult to be executed reliably every time.	Doubtful
Complexity	A process composed of many elements breaks down when novel interactions take place.	Rarely
Uncertainty	Lacking sufficient knowledge of future events, people take reasonable actions that nonetheless produce undesired results.	No
Hypothesis-testing experiment	An experiment conducted to test a prediction that a particular design or course of action will produce a particular result fails to confirm the hypothesis.	No
Exploratory experiment	An experiment conducted to expand knowledge and investigate a possibility leads to an undesired result.	No

I've shared this spectrum of causes with executives from a range of industries and asked them to estimate what percentage of the failures in their organization might be caused by blameworthy actions. Usually, they pick a number that is less than 5 percent. Then I ask how often failures in their company are actually treated as blameworthy. After a pause (or an uncomfortable laugh), they come up with a much higher number, say 70 to 90 percent. The discrepancy (between less than 5 and 90) is a far greater problem than most managers realize. If thoughtful managers understand that failures do happen, and that it's rare when an individual can rightly be blamed, then they'll also see that to engage in blaming is more than just illogical. It's counterproductive.

Why? Because valuable failures go unreported. Failure's lessons are lost. The real cost of blaming people for bad outcomes—when the real causes are uncertainty or complexity, for example—is that innovation is hampered. To understand this better, let's take a look at three kinds of failure.

Mapping the Failure Landscape

Although an infinite number of things can go wrong in organizations, they fall into three broad categories of failure: preventable, complexity-related, and intelligent. The causes discussed above correspond roughly, and in sets of three, to these three failure types. In this book, we are particularly interested in intelligent failures at the frontier (the frontier being where innovation occurs). But intelligent failures are best understood by contrasting them to the other types.

Preventable failures. Most failures in this category can indeed be considered "bad" in the sense that they were highly preventable. They may involve unwarranted deviation from a well-defined process in a routine operation. In fact, they are particularly relevant in the context of routine operations; that is, when knowledge for how to do things "right" is available. Although rarely deliberate, such deviations are almost always avoidable. With proper training and support, steps in a routine process can and should be followed consistently. Failure to do so is usually due to one of the first three of the nine reasons for failure in the spectrum (violation, inattention, or lack of ability). When that happens, the causes can be readily identified and solutions developed.

One approach to avoiding preventable failures is the much celebrated Toyota Production System, which builds continuous learning from tiny failures (small process deviations) into its systematic approach to improvement.

As most students of operations know well, team members on a Toyota assembly line who spot a problem, or even a potential problem, are encouraged to pull a rope called the "Andon Cord," which immediately initiates a problem-solving process. (The Japanese word *andon* is a type of lantern and, in manufacturing, a visual signal.) Production continues unimpeded if the problem is successfully remedied in less than a minute. Otherwise, production is halted—despite the substantial loss of revenue a line stoppage creates—until the failure is understood and resolved. That way, longer-term profits are built through the production of high-quality products that build customer loyalty.

In innovation projects, experiments that have been run before and failed but are inadvertently run again qualify as preventable failures. Optimal practice for innovation is not to avoid failure, but it does avoid producing the same failure twice.

Complex failures. Many organizational failures are the result of system complexity and are not completely preventable. When a particular combination of needs, people, and problems has never occurred before—such as triaging patients in a hospital emergency room, troubleshooting in a major IT installation, or running a fast-growing start-up—at least some small failures must be expected. To assume otherwise would be illogical. System failure also is a perpetual risk in complex organizations like aircraft carriers, nuclear power plants, and air traffic control.

While serious failures may be averted by following risk-management best practices, including a thorough analysis of all near-miss events (as discussed in "Learn Fast"), small process failures will inevitably occur. To consider them "bad" is a misunderstanding of how complex systems work. It is also counterproductive. It blocks the rapid identification and correction of small failures that is crucial to avoiding consequential failures. The majority of failures experienced by hospitalized patients—massive heparin overdoses that harmed babies in two separate hospitals a few years ago, for instance— occur as a result of a series of small process failures that unfortunately line up in just the wrong way to allow a patient to be harmed. Best practice means catching and correcting these small failures before this happens, because, again, small failures will occur in complex, customized work. Major failures, however, can be prevented through vigilance, good communication, and proactive learning. (For all of these behaviors, of course, psychological safety is critical.)

Intelligent failures. The most important insight for managers seeking to promote innovation is that failures in this category aren't in fact "bad" at all. Indeed, intelligent failures can rightly be considered "good." They provide valuable new knowledge that can help a team to come up with innovative products and help a company to grow. Intelligent failures occur when experimentation is necessary—when answers are not knowable in advance (because we've never been in this exact situation before and probably never will again). Discovering and testing new drugs, creating a radically new business, developing a new biofuel, creating a prototype for an energy-efficient vehicle, and testing customer reactions in a new market are examples of undertakings where this is the case. These are tasks that demand intelligent failure. And the faster the failures happen, the better.

This kind of experimentation is often referred to as *trial and error*, but that is a misnomer. "Error" implies that you could have done it right the first time and that not doing so constitutes a mistake. But a trial is needed precisely when results are not knowable in advance. For this reason, I call the experimentation process *trial and failure*. (We lack a word that means "unpreventable novel failures," which itself is telling.)

Failing Well—At the Right Scale

When you're exploring the frontier, the right kind of experimentation is one that produces good failures quickly and intelligently, which is why Professor Sim Sitkin at Duke calls them *intelligent failures*, despite the apparent oxymoron.[34] Managers who work with failures in this fashion are more likely to get the most out of them—and also to avoid the *unintelligent* failure of conducting experiments on a scale that is larger than necessary.

As an example, in the late 1990s a major telecommunications company I'll refer to as Telco set out to innovate.[35] To be positioned at what was then the forefront of new and somewhat unproven technology, Telco decided to launch digital subscriber line technology, or DSL, to provide its customers with high-speed internet service. In its well-intentioned desire to innovate, however, Telco made the mistake of experimenting at too large a scale.

Despite the very real operational risks of the unproven new technology, Telco launched DSL throughout its entire market, all at once, and before the company was really able to deliver it reliably. The outcome, unfortunately, was a dismal failure. Customer satisfaction, normally in the high 80s, dove down to the teens. As many as five hundred customers a day were waiting to hear back about some aspect of service. Twenty percent of complaints were taking 30 or more days to resolve. Customers were frustrated and angry, and employee morale suffered as well.

Of course, Telco's mistake did not lie in trying to innovate, or even in experiencing failure as part of the innovation process. The mistake was that it launched an experiment—an uncertain new service operation—at such a large and painful scale. By rolling DSL out to the entire market, rather than launching a small pilot that could help it see what worked (and what didn't), Telco lost the chance to make rapid changes as a result of thoughtful experimentation. The company converted what could have been an intelligent failure into a pre-ventable (not so intelligent) failure. At that point in time, the process knowledge for how to deliver the new service reliably across diverse customer situations was simply underdeveloped. Not considering this mismatch, Telco was in a position of managing an initiative that should have been treated as a complex new operation, not as a routine operation.

In contrast, IDEO, the global product-design consul-tancy, set out to launch a new kind of innovation-strategy service.[36] Traditionally, IDEO helped clients design new products within their existing product lines. The new service would assist clients in identifying new strategic product line opportunities. Knowing it had not worked out all the details for delivering the new services effectively, IDEO started with a small project with a low-tech manufacturing client, so as to learn from an early small experiment. Although the project failed—the client did not change its product strategy—IDEO learned from it. The company then figured out what it had to do differently, including developing new processes for understanding clients' businesses, and hiring staff with MBAs who had experience diagnosing and developing business strategy. Today, strategic services account for more than a third of IDEO's revenues.

We can sing the praises of intelligent failure as much as we want. But that inner child, the one that wants to be right and is terrified of being wrong, doesn't just go gently into that good night. That's where leadership comes in.

Leading Failure

As we've seen, failing well means tolerating unavoidable process failures in complex systems and celebrating intelligent failures at the frontier of knowledge. Rather than promoting mediocrity, such tolerance is essential for any team or organization seeking the new knowledge that failure in complex and novel settings provides.

Strategically producing failures takes this one step further. Researchers in basic science know that once in a great while an experiment yields a spectacular success. However, more often (far more often!) experiments result in failure. Scientists can't succeed unless they learn to recognize failure as a step on the path to success. Recognizing this, the chief scientific officer at pharmaceutical giant Eli Lilly throws failure parties to celebrate clinical trials or scientific programs that were intelligent but that nonetheless failed. This odd ritual makes scientists more willing to take intelligent risks, but it also encourages them to speak up sooner rather than later about a failing course of action. Failing is neither blameworthy nor shameful, but part of a valiant effort to generate new knowledge.

Most managers in business, however, feel a great deal of pressure to make sure that their product or service is perfect when it goes out into the world. This pressure affects the pilot projects that are designed to test the new idea. Managers are so eager to succeed (understandably!) that they often design pilots that incorporate optimal conditions rather than representative ones. The result? Fragile successes. A pilot is meant to generate knowledge about what won't work, not simply affirm the genius behind an innovation. Pilots must be designed to fail.

To understand why, consider the Telco failure again. Before the full-scale urban launch, managers had run a small pilot in a suburb that housed well-educated, tech-savvy customers. The pilot was considered a soaring success. Unfortunately, pilot conditions were anything but representative of the large and diverse urban market in which the full-scale launch would take place. To make matters worse, the pilot was staffed by particularly expert and friendly service reps who were well versed in the new technology and could make it work for any customer's home computer setup. This small pilot was not so much a hypothesis-testing experiment as a demonstration project. It was designed to succeed—rather than to fail intelligently so that the subsequent full-scale launch could be a success.

What should Telco have done? First, the technology should have been tested in a small and unsophisticated market (old computers, fewer tech-savvy customers), with normal staffing levels to support it. The pilot should have been designed to uncover every little thing that could possibly go wrong—before announcing the new service to all customers. Managers would have been poised to reward intelligent failures and to help teams learn from them quickly to improve the product as well as the service that accompanied it. To generalize this lesson, Exhibit 1 lists a few questions that should be answered in the affirmative when designing the right kind of pilot projects—the kind that fail intelligently.

As the questions in Exhibit 1 demonstrate, managers hoping to successfully launch an innovative or novel product should not try to produce success the first time around. Instead, they should attempt to design and execute

Exhibit 1.   Failing Well in Effective Pilot Projects[37]

Managers of successful pilots must be able to answer "yes" to the following questions:

- Is the pilot program being tested under typical circumstances instead of optimal conditions?
- Are the employees, customers, and resources representative of the firm's real operating environment?
- Is the goal of the pilot to learn as much as possible rather than demonstrate to senior managers the value of the new system?
- Is the goal of learning as much as possible understood by everyone involved, including employees and managers?
- Is it clear that compensation and performance ratings are not based on a successful outcome of the pilot?
- Were explicit changes made as a result of the pilot program?

---

the most informative "trial-and-failure" process possible. This strategy for learning from *pilot-size failures* is a way to ensure that full-scale, online services will succeed.

Courage and Fear

Like the cowardly lion in *The Wizard of Oz*, we have to learn that fear and courage exist side by side. The lion didn't understand at first that courage does not mean an absence of fear, but a willingness to act in spite of fear.

Confronting failure means confronting our imperfection. This takes courage because, of course, it is unpleasant. But acknowledging our limits with good nature and a sense of humor allows us to get on with things, to be creative and innovative. Environments that discourage the reporting of problems, mistakes, and failures block this forward movement, this learning. Managers who ask employees to be brave and to speak up must not later express disapproval or even anger. Rather, gratitude is called for when an employee reveals the complex systems at work behind organizational failures. Then the real innovation can begin.

Managers are often concerned, as I've mentioned, that embracing failure will create a messy, anarchic, anything-goes environment in which nothing ever gets done. But this simply isn't the case. One does not follow from the other. The fact is, failure is inevitable, especially in today's complex knowledge economy. Learning from failure, even moving in that direction, will give any organization a competitive edge.

Tom Kelley (general manager of IDEO) and David Kelley (founder and chairman) have written about the importance of what they call "creative confidence": "the natural ability to come up with new ideas and the courage to try them out."[38] They put this into action in their company by giving employees "strategies to get past four fears that hold most of us back: fear of the messy unknown, fear of being judged, fear of the first step, and fear of losing control."

No matter what kind of failure occurs, avoid playing the blame game—the pull to name culprits rather than causes. This game is deeply counterproductive. Get comfortable with the mind-set that identifies failure as an inevitable, valuable part of the innovation journey.

Of course, failure is not worth much if we don't learn from it (and learn fast!). Let's look at what it takes to do that well.

Learn Fast

In companies, learning fast is a team sport. Although individual employees learn in a casual way all the time (having new insights, improving their skills), this type of learning doesn't automatically help the company to perform better. Individual participation in formal training programs doesn't either. Here, we look at what it takes for organizations to systematically learn from the vast array of experiences they have—especially from failure.

Everyone agrees that people and organizations should learn from failure. And yet organizations that systematically and effectively learn from failure are very rare. This is because learning fast requires discipline. It is systematic and effortful. I will explicate four steps of the learning process that underlies innovation.[39] Of course, there are barriers to learning inherent in each of these steps and we'll take a look at how some companies overcome them. Finally, I'll give some tips for leading learning in the context of innovation.

Deliberate learning from experience starts with the right managerial mind-set. I call it *organizing to learn.*[40] It's a way of thinking and acting that is driven by the recognition that the world keeps changing, and that today's answers are almost certainly not tomorrow's. It means not having too much (unwarranted) faith in our first round of ideas. For instance, recall the Telco DSL launch described earlier. Senior management's (unsubstantiated) faith in the company's ability to deliver led to a premature full-scale rollout in a large and diverse urban market.

Learning as You Go

The Telco failure happened because the company went all out with an innovation without accurately assessing its own current operational capabilities. Imagine that instead of a full-scale, widely advertised rollout, Telco had engaged a few pioneering customers who tolerated some imperfections in the brand-new service and also gave the company feedback to help it improve the service quickly. As co-investigators, these pioneers might have even enjoyed helping the company find the weak spots. Together, company and customer would learn as they went. Before long, the problems would be solved and the kinks worked out in an inevitable march toward a reliable, easy-to-use innovation, which future customers would take for granted. As one might roll out a carpet, a *rollout* implies that something is ready to go, just needing a bit of momentum to propel it forward. *Cycling out*, by contrast, is a journey punctuated with deliberate and thoughtful iteration and learning.

Any company trying to innovate must figure out a way to learn as quickly as possible from early experiences (preferably at a small scale) in the life of the project. There are no shortcuts. To provide a compelling new product or service that works and appeals to a wide range of customers, you have to be willing to start with one that *doesn't* work well. It means taking seriously the adage of nineteenth-century British philosopher G. K. Chesterton: "If something's worth doing, it's worth doing *badly*."[41] Of course, just doing something badly (before you figure out how to do it well) isn't enough. To learn fast from experience, managers have to deliberately frame the early-stage experiences as *experiments*. Experiments generate data—and data must be learned from.

On the innovation journey, each step is an experiment, and each experiment must be different from the one before. Its design must incorporate the knowledge gained in the prior cycle. In this way, an innovation cycles out, bumpily, improving as it expands. For example, Netflix introduced its Watch Instantly offering in successive waves of 250,000 customers, taking six months to cycle out its instant downloading technology; during this time, the company constantly checked in with customers via follow-up emails that inquired about the quality of specific movies watched.[42] It also set up and actively monitored a Netflix blog to explain operations, step by step, and to respond to frequent customer posts regarding problems, requests, and suggestions. The service was essentially free for several years, until the problems were worked out. Once it really worked smoothly, Netflix asked customers to pay. This is the kind of practice that companies use to learn fast. Above all, innovation requires companies to *fully utilize employee and customer experiences for learning.*

How to Learn Fast

Learning in general, and especially for innovation, involves four essential steps: *diagnosing* the situation, challenge, or problem (including assessing what is currently known about it), *designing* initial actions, *taking action* (viewed as experimenting), and *reflecting* to gain the lessons from the experiment.

Diagnosis

Diagnosis involves sizing up the situation and the challenges that might lie ahead. It's about identifying the opportunities for innovation—the subtle customer desires or pain points that haven't yet been addressed by viable products or services. Diagnosis may range from extended study of customer behaviors to behind-the-scenes analysis of large data sets, to a quick exchange of ideas between colleagues about opportunities.

At Intuit, the financial software company, engineers directly observe customers as they interact with the software, so as to evaluate how easy or difficult it is for them to use the features built into the product.[43] This allows engineers to observe unmet user needs firsthand, needs that customers themselves lack either the experience or the vocabulary to voice. Another part of diagnosis for innovation is assessing what's feasible, given the current state of technology or the costs of inputs. Opportunities may be wide, but they are not infinite.

Design

The next step is to identify possibilities for action. Design is done when a team has a preliminary commitment to action—whether through a formal decision or plan, or by a gradual shift into agreement to try something out. The purpose of design in innovation is to guide action. That may sound oversimple, but design fosters learning by making action more deliberate and conscious.

At Motorola, one of the most successful innovations in the company's history was the RAZR phone, introduced back in 2004.[44] That innovation was the result of a motivated team's efforts to brainstorm shapes and features for the phone and then to quickly try out mockups made of clay before getting too far down the path with real materials. As in this example, the design step in any innovation journey is often just a starting point. It may lead to only a single step forward, one that we expect to revise as soon as we learn more. Thus, in an innovation project, a focus group might be used to react to an experimental new service or product idea before we figure out all of the details of execution.

Action, or Experimentation

The shift from talking to doing, from considering to trying, also happens in teams. A key to effective action in execution-as-learning is making sure to track what actually happens as well as tracking the results of the action. Traditional management controls emphasize *outcome* data, which capture results. Execution-as-learning pays just as much attention to *process* data, which describe how work unfolds.

Rapid, unconstrained action is at the heart of innovation. It's called experimentation. Scientists, of course, routinely experiment, hoping to be first to make an important discovery in the process. Experiments range from those for which possible outcomes are all but unknown in advance to those in which strong hypotheses are being tested. In basic research, a scientist who has a 70 percent failure rate in the experiments she runs might be in the process of earning a Nobel Prize. The RAZR team tried out several configurations before hitting on its revolutionary slimming design, by putting the battery next to the circuit board (prior phones had them stacked) to reduce thickness. Teams at IDEO routinely build quick prototypes to see what new products might look like in three dimensions.[45] The point is simply to try things and see what happens. It's easy to stay in the conceptual plane—to talk about ideas and possibilities forever. *A key to successful innovation is making frequent, small forays into action.*

Reflection

After taking action, it's critical to take some time to understand what happened; what worked and what didn't. Reflection is about digging into failures, intelligent or otherwise. It's an analytic task.

Innovation teams have to learn fast from the trials and failures they produce so that they can conduct new trials as soon as possible. Reflecting on failure is rarely fun, but it's essential to figuring out the true causes of a failure in order to determine what gets tried next. Don't shortchange reflection in the desire to move quickly to the next experiment, because high-quality reflection can help avoid predictable failures in subsequent actions. Ed Catmull, founder and president of Pixar, lamented that Pixar employees would just as soon avoid post-project reflection altogether, preferring to relish the success of a film than to stop and identify what could have gone better. To get more out of this critical step, he instituted the following: participants are asked to list five things they would do again, and then to discuss five things they wouldn't do. According to Catmull, this positive-negative balance created a safe environment conducive to discussing every aspect of a project thoughtfully.[46]

It's not easy for any company facing cost constraints (and who isn't!) to stop and reflect. Disciplined evaluation takes productive resources off-line, and conventional management wisdom views this as lost productivity. Nonetheless, the only way to achieve and sustain excellence is for leaders to insist that their organizations invest resources in the reflection that makes innovation possible.

Overcoming Barriers to Learning

Learning from failure is a hallmark of innovative companies. But it requires an unusual mind-set and systematic effort, and companies that do it well are rare. Why? Because there are barriers to innovation at each step of the learning process.

Barriers to Diagnosis

Diagnosis sets the stage for learning from the inevitable failures in any innovation process. This is where opportunities are assessed and aspirational goals are revisited (remember "Aim High"). Because most people experience strong negative feelings around failure, these kinds of conversations must be managed thoughtfully.

Consider Alan Mulally's leadership at Ford.[47] Shortly after arriving from Boeing as Ford's new CEO in September 2006, Mulally instituted a system for detecting failure. He asked managers to color-code their reports green for good, yellow for caution, and red for problems—a common management technique. According to a 2009 story in *Fortune*, at his first few meetings all of the managers coded their operations green, much to Mulally's frustration. Reminding them that the company had lost several billion dollars the previous year, he asked straight out, "Isn't anything not going well?"[48] After one tentative yellow report was made about a serious product defect that would probably delay a launch, Mulally responded to the ensuing deathly silence with applause. After that—particularly after other executives discovered that the first messenger of bad news hadn't been fired or demoted—weekly staff meetings were full of color.

This story illustrates a pervasive and fundamental problem. Although many methods of surfacing current and pending failures exist, they are grossly underutilized in today's organizations. For instance, total quality management (TQM) and soliciting feedback from customers are well-known techniques for bringing failures to light. But too many messengers—even the most senior executives—are reluctant to convey bad news to bosses and colleagues. For example, a senior executive I knew in a large consumer products company had grave reservations about a takeover already in the works when he joined the management team. Conscious of his newcomer status, he was silent in discussions about the plan, because all the other executives were so enthusiastic. Many months later, when the takeover had clearly failed, the team gathered to review what had happened. With the help of a consultant, each executive considered what he or she might have done to contribute to the failure. The newcomer, openly apologetic about his past silence, explained that he hadn't wanted to be "the skunk at the picnic."[49]

It's just not possible to diagnose or predict failure when people don't feel it is safe to express their full thoughts and feelings about the various issues on the table. Leaders have to go out of their way to avoid "shooting the messenger," and to instead encourage people to speak up. Mulally's applause is a great example of how to do that. People must feel able to speak up about both clear and ambiguous signals that something might be amiss. This is essential to innovation! Without evidence that the present is deficient in some way, the motivation to innovate is lacking.

Barriers to Design

For the purposes of organizational learning, the design step is a thoughtful pause that guides subsequent action. The most important barrier to design is a lack of psychological safety. When people are overly worried about what others will think of them, they become reluctant to raise potentially crazy ideas. But innovation benefits from crazy ideas. Sometimes it's the crazy idea—despite being impractical or useless in its own right—that triggers someone else to have a truly innovative and useable idea. It's important in innovation to make sure people feel uninhibited to dream and imagine all sorts of possibilities.

This points to a second barrier. Beyond feeling safe to speak up, people also have to re-engage their imaginations, which can sometimes atrophy in corporate hierarchies. A lack of imagination is another important barrier to coming up with designs for action that are new enough—enough of a departure from the status quo—to generate worthwhile experiments. An important leadership task, therefore, is to provoke and nurture imagination, to help people think as broadly as possible about options. Thinking is free—whereas action can be expensive. So the design step should be used to conduct thought experiments through which obviously wrong-headed approaches can be skipped going forward.

Barriers to Action and Experimentation

A lack of psychological safety is also a barrier to the third step in the learning process—deliberate experimentation. If people don't feel safe, they will conduct only very low-risk experiments, where successful outcomes are relatively easy to predict. (This is why managers sometimes conduct pilots that don't yield much information, as described earlier in the examination of what it takes to "Fail Well.") But innovative organizations are willing to conduct (and learn quickly from) experiments that fail.

Consider the example of IDEO, the design firm, which promotes internal experimentation through slogans such as, "Fail often in order to succeed sooner," and "Enlightened trial-and-error succeeds over the planning of the lone genius." These statements are accompanied by frequent small experiments, and much good humor over the associated failures. Recall that 3M (in the Introduction) also encourages deliberate experiments and celebrates intelligent failure, giving rise to decades of successful product innovation.

In many companies, incentives (formal and informal) are inconsistent with stated values about learning from failure. This makes true experimentation difficult and rare. This obvious barrier to experimentation must be mitigated—by aligning incentives with what it takes to innovate. Those who experiment should be celebrated, and companies must publicize both failures and successes internally, so that all employees can see that the idea of learning from failure is more than just "talk."

A final barrier to effective experimentation is the reluctance people have to call an experiment a failure, even after the data are clearly pointing in that direction. It's important to teach people when to declare defeat in an experimental course of action. The human tendency to hope for the best and avoid failure at all costs gets in the way, and organizational hierarchies exacerbate the problem. As a result, failing R&D projects are often kept going much longer than is analytically rational or economically prudent. We throw good money after bad, praying that we'll pull a rabbit out of a hat. Intuition and experience may tell engineers or scientists that a project has fatal flaws, but the formal decision to call it a failure may be delayed for months.[50]

Barriers to Reflection

Organizations cannot learn from failure, and other experiences, without thoughtful analysis and discussion. Again, a lack of psychological safety can be a major barrier to doing this well. Formal processes or forums for discussing, analyzing, and applying the lessons of failure involve direct language and straightforward confrontation of sometimes unwelcome facts. People rarely do this well unless they feel psychologically safe enough to leave their ego at the door and fully engage with the substance of the discussion.

A second major barrier (as we've seen) is blame. After experiencing failure, people typically blame other people or forces beyond their control (like traffic and weather). We tend to downplay our own responsibility and blame external or situational factors when we fail, only to do the reverse when assessing the failures of others—a psychological trap known as fundamental attribution error. Leaders have to help groups avoid the blame game and keep attention focused on what can be learned from the prior action or experiment and what that means for the next one. Expert outside (or internal) facilitators can keep a reflection process productive and bring new perspectives and insights that deepen the analysis.

Effective analysis of failure requires both time and space, along with skill in managing the conflicting perspectives that may emerge. Some organizations, like the military, set aside time for "after-action reviews"; hospitals use "morbidity and mortality" (M&M) conferences to discuss significant mistakes or unexpected patient deaths as a forum for identifying, discussing, and learning from failures.[51]

A third barrier is lack of technical or analytic skill.[52] To learn from failed or successful experiments, people need to know how to use basic scientific tools, including the appropriate use of statistical analyses or qualitative data analysis. Relying exclusively on common sense, gut feel, or intuition can lead to flawed conclusions. Even without meaning to, we all favor evidence that supports our existing beliefs over alternative explanations. This is known as the confirmation bias.[53]

The final barrier is emotional. As previously noted, examining any failure is likely to be emotionally unpleasant. Left to our own devices, most of us will speed through or avoid failure analysis altogether. Reflection takes skill and patience. Yet many managers admire and are rewarded for decisiveness, efficiency, and action—not thoughtful reflection. It takes leadership to push forward against this cultural tide, ensuring that lessons are learned. In the long run, this saves time and promotes the innovation that is so necessary for tomorrow's success.

The goal in reflection is to go beyond first-order reasons (procedures weren't followed) to find second- and third-order explanations for a failure. One way to do this is to use interdisciplinary teams with diverse skills and perspectives. Complex failures in particular are the result of multiple events that occurred in different departments or disciplines or at different levels of the organization. Understanding what happened and how to prevent it from happening again requires detailed, team-based discussion and analysis. Although this takes patience and skill, the benefits for innovation are well worth the investment of managerial effort.

Leading Learning to Innovate

Overcoming the barriers to learning in the pursuit of innovation requires openness, transparency, and, yes, psychological safety. Leaders who wish to promote innovation must work to create and reinforce a culture that counteracts the blame game and makes people feel comfortable with and responsible for surfacing failures and learning from them. The leader's role is to insist on a clear understanding of what happened—not to ask "Who did it?"—when things go wrong.

Framing for Learning

Leaders should also send the right message about the nature of the work, such as reminding people in R&D, "We're in the discovery business, and the faster we fail, the faster we'll succeed." Many managers don't understand or appreciate this subtle but crucial point. To build a culture that is conducive to innovation, managers must create an environment in which everyone can put aside self-protective defenses and approach the work with curiosity and a desire to learn from failure. We cannot underestimate the psychological and interpersonal barriers to this organizational-learning process. Reframing failure from something associated with shame and weakness to something that is linked to risk, uncertainty, and improvement is a critical step in the learning journey.[54]

Repeat (Learning Never Stops)

The secret to organizational learning and innovation, as noted way back in the Introduction, is that the learning cycle never stops. Once the purpose (where the team is headed) has been established, the process (how we get there) can nearly always be improved.

Team sports have guidelines that move the game forward. Reflection, sharing insights widely in a psychologically safe environment, creating the next experiment, and learning from failures are all crucial steps that move innovation forward. In "Aim High" and "Team Up," we described how to establish a goal and a process. In "Learn Fast," we looked at how to continuously improve that process to move closer to the goal. Eventually, learning continuously from failure should become second nature—but for now let's just say that it's far more systematic and structured than it might first appear.

In organizations that innovate, learning must become a habit.

Conclusion

Teaming to innovate, as many of the examples in this book illustrate, is fueled by a commitment to create a better world in some small or large way. The size of the contribution depends on the kind of work you do and the kind of organization you work in. But no matter where you work, setting out to innovate is an act of hope.

It is my hope that this short book will help you succeed in your quest to innovate. Toward that end, this conclusion pulls out the key ideas and recommendations that support each aspect of the teaming-to-innovate journey, and closes with a few reflections about the essential qualities of leaders who help make it happen.

Recommendations for a Successful Innovation Journey

Aim High

- *Aspire to change something.* Articulate a meaningful, aspirational goal—one that connects in some way to making the world a better place, whether through appealing products and services that improve customers' lives or through solutions to vexing problems.
- *Touch hearts and minds.* Goals that best motivate innovation appeal to both reason and emotion: they make sense for the organization, and they resonate emotionally with the people who will work hard to achieve them.
- *Stretch!* Worthy goals are challenging, but not impossible. If a goal seems completely out of reach, people are less motivated and often feel less able to speak up honestly. Alternatively, if a goal isn't aspirational enough, innovation may not be required to achieve it.
- *Make it safe.* When setting a goal for innovation, make sure it's clear that you want to hear back from people. Open dialogue is vital to fleshing out and taking ownership of a goal. A climate of psychological safety to talk about problems and raise ideas is essential to getting people lined up behind a shared goal.

- *Inquire*. Use inquiry to invite others to help develop and take ownership of the shared goal.

Team Up

- *Ensure diversity*. Reach out to bring people together from different functions, professions, locations, or other organizational groups. Innovation comes from new combinations of ideas and skills.
- *Cross boundaries*. Diversity can only be put to good use when people actively cross boundaries to find out what's on the other side. People should be encouraged to cross disciplinary, distance, and status boundaries.
- *Nurture curiosity*. Build and reinforce the kind of curiosity that drives boundary-crossers to engage in mutual learning.
- *Make it safe*. Psychological safety plays a critical role throughout the innovation journey. Teaming up can only happen fully and effectively if people feel safe enough to open up and share their ideas, their hopes, and their concerns.
- *Provide process guidelines*. Teaming goes well when people follow process discipline to remind themselves to check in with each other, moving through phases of listening, learning, sharing, empathizing, and creating together.

- *Put conflict to good use*. Conflicting ideas lie at the heart of innovation, but conflict can trigger strong emotions and negative interpersonal attributes. Manage conflict carefully by practicing self-awareness, leading thoughtful conversations, and building resilient relationships.

Fail Well

- *Stop the blame game*. The causes of failure range from deliberate violations to thoughtful experiments that yield unexpected results. In organizations, failures that are actually caused by blameworthy acts are rare. Yet the common spontaneous response is to treat failures as if someone were to blame. Closing this gap is key to building a culture of innovation.
- *Distinguish three types of failure*. Not all failures are created equal. Some are preventable, some are complex, and some are even intelligent.
- *Motivate intelligent failures*. Failing well often is the key to rapid innovation.
- *Fail at the right scale*. Don't bet the company on an uncertain new idea. Test it out at a small scale and learn fast from what works and, more important, from what doesn't.
- *Make it safe*. Innovative organizations are marked by a palpable climate of psychological safety that rewards intelligent failure.

Learn Fast

- *Be deliberate about the four steps of the learning process:* diagnose, design, act, reflect.
- *Be aware of barriers at each step.* The barriers to diagnosing, designing, acting, and reflecting can be overcome by leaders paying attention to process and to what people are trying to learn fast in different steps of the process.
- *Framing for learning.* Most people take for granted an execution-oriented frame for getting work done. Reframing the work as a learning process is an essential driver of innovation.

Repeat

- *Keep on going.* Reinforce your passionate commitment to innovation and learning, fueled by key leadership qualities.

Leaders Who Innovate

A few qualities that serve leaders well on an innovation journey deserve special attention: imagination, curiosity, courage, flexibility, discipline, and perseverance.

Imagination. To begin with, *aiming high* is an act of imagination. By its very nature, coming up with new possibilities requires imagination—or better yet, the ability to nurture it in others. We all were imaginative as children. Now it's time to re-engage and reinforce this innate attribute.

Curiosity. To innovate, people must be deeply interested in what others have to offer, no matter what their status or formal position in the hierarchy. Getting to know people from different backgrounds and disciplines quickly—people who speak different languages (culturally and professionally)—means listening to other points of view, checking one's understanding, and integrating new information into what you see and do. Of course this requires skillful inquiry too, but curiosity is the driving force behind both teaming and innovation. When you're curious, inquiry is a natural and spontaneous act. And genuine inquiry is a gift to others.

Courage. Innovation is a risky business. And risk calls for courage. You have to be able to say what you think, to change your mind, to experiment. This is why it's so important to build a culture of psychological safety. Even then, in designing and executing the experiments that enable innovation, you need courage, knowing full well that many of them will fail.

Flexibility. Innovation is a fluid process, an uncertain journey. You don't always know in advance what will be expected of you. Flexibility—the capacity to change course, entertain new ideas, admit failure, and try something else—is essential.

Discipline. To innovate effectively, learning has to happen fast, not just because the competition is trying to innovate too, but also because your resources are not infinite. Fast learning is disciplined learning. It might look chaotic, but the learning that happens in the most innovative companies is systematic and disciplined.

Oh, and one other thing belongs on this list: the *perseverance* to start all over again.

Notes

1. See A. C. Edmondson. *Teaming: How Organizations Learn, Innovate, and Compete in the Knowledge Economy.* San Francisco: Jossey-Bass, 2012.
2. For a detailed case study on Danone's approach to knowledge sharing, see A. C. Edmondson and D. Lane. "Global Knowledge Management at Danone (A) (Abridged)." Harvard Business School Case 613–003, July 2012. (Revised from original July 2012 version), 1.
3. A. C. Edmondson and K. S. Roloff. "Phase Zero: Introducing New Services at IDEO (B)." Harvard Business School Supplement 606–123, March 2013. (Revised from original June 2006 version).
4. A. C. Edmondson, S. Ribot, and T. Zuzul. "Designing a Culture of Collaboration at Lake Nona Medical City." Harvard Business School Case 613–022, October 2012.

5. A. C. Edmondson, S. Ribot, and T. Zuzul. "Designing a Culture of Collaboration at Lake Nona Medical City." Harvard Business School Case 613–022, October 2012.

6. A. C. Edmondson. *Teaming: How Organizations Learn, Innovate, and Compete in the Knowledge Economy*. San Francisco: Jossey-Bass, 2012.

7. Ibid.

8. Table 1 is reproduced from A. C. Edmondson. *Teaming: How Organizations Learn, Innovate, and Compete in the Knowledge Economy*. San Francisco: Jossey-Bass, 2012, 11–43.

9. A. Tucker and A. C. Edmondson. "Why Hospitals Don't Learn from Failures: Organizational and Psychological Dynamics That Inhibit System Change." *California Management Review* 45, no. 2 (Winter), 2003.

10. A. C. Edmondson. *Teaming: How Organizations Learn, Innovate, and Compete in the Knowledge Economy*. San Francisco: Jossey-Bass, 2012, 11–43.

11. Ibid.

12. J. Smith. "What to Do When You Don't Hear Back from a Job Interview?" *Forbes* online, February 20, 2013. http://www.forbes.com/sites/jacquelynsmith/2013/02/20/what-to-do-when-you-dont-hear-back-after-a-job-interview/ (accessed June 21, 2013).

13. F. Rashid, H. Leonard, and A. C. Edmondson. "Chilean Mining Rescue (A)." Harvard Business School Case 612–046, 2012; and A. C. Edmondson. *Teaming: How Organizations Learn, Innovate and Compete in the Knowledge Economy*. San Francisco: Jossey-Bass, 2012, 185–217.

14. F. Rashid, H. Leonard, and A. C. Edmondson. "Chilean Mining Rescue (A)." Harvard Business School Case

612–046, 2012; and F. Rashid, H. Leonard, and A. C. Edmondson. "Chilean Mining Rescue (B)." Harvard Business School Case 612–47, 2012.

15. A. C. Edmondson, M. Roberto, and A. Tucker. "Children's Hospital and Clinics." Harvard Business School Case 9–302–50, 2002; and A. C. Edmondson. *Teaming: How Organizations Learn, Innovate and Compete in the Knowledge Economy.* San Francisco: Jossey-Bass, 2012, 257–87.

16. A. C. Edmondson, M. Roberto, and A. Tucker. "Children's Hospital and Clinics." Harvard Business School Case 9–302–050, 2002, 4.

17. Ibid.

18. M. A. Carey and C. Weaver. "New 'Innovation' Chief Comes from 'Model' Health Care System." *Kaiser Health News,* September 28, 2010. http://www.kaiserhealthnews. org/stories/2010/september/28/cms-innovation-office-health-reform.aspx.

19. R. Gilfillan. "Speech at Healthcare Innovation Summit." YouTube video, 17:36, June 20, 2011. http://www.youtube.com/watch?v=RPQEG0Dfg30.

20. T. Dwyer. "TRMC Is Building for the Future." *The Messenger,* January 27, 2013. http://www.kaiserhealthnews.org/stories/2010/september/28/cms-innovation-office-health-reform.aspx.

21. For additional details, see A. C. Edmondson and J. Tachau. "'Argo': The CIA's Mission Impossible in Iran." Harvard Business School Case 613–087, April 2013.

22. Ibid.

23. A. C. Edmondson. *Teaming: How Organizations Learn, Innovate and Compete in the Knowledge Economy.* San Francisco: Jossey-Bass, 2012, 185–217.

24. This example is found in A. C. Edmondson. *Teaming: How Organizations Learn, Innovate and Compete in the Knowledge Economy*. San Francisco: Jossey-Bass, 2012, 195.

25. Ibid.

26. S. Thompson. "Trinity Accountable Care Organization Is an Asset." *The Messenger*, December 30, 2012. http://www.messengernews.net/page/content.detail/id/553715/Trinity-Accountable-Care-Organization-is-an-asset.html (accessed June 21, 2013).

27. Ibid.; and R. G. Eccles, A. C. Edmondson, and D. Karadzhova. "Arup: Building the Water Cube." Harvard Business School Case 410–054, June 2010.

28. E. Schein. *Organizational Culture and Leadership*. 4th ed. San Francisco: Jossey-Bass, 2010, 155–76 (ch. 21).

29. A. C. Edmondson and D. M. Smith. "Too Hot to Handle? How to Manage Relationship Conflict." *California Management Review* 49, no. 1 (Fall), 2006: 6–31.

30. J. Metcalfe and W. Mischel. "A Hot/Cool System of Delay of Gratification: Dynamics of Willpower." *Psychological Review* 106, no. 1, 1999: 3–19.

31. A. C. Edmondson and D. M. Smith. "Too Hot to Handle? How to Manage Relationship Conflict." *California Management Review* 49, no. 1 (Fall), 2006: 6–31.

32. A. C. Edmondson. "Strategies for Learning from Failure." *Harvard Business Review* 89, no. 4, 2011; A. C. Edmondson. *Teaming: How Organizations Learn, Innovate and Compete in the Knowledge Economy*. San Francisco: Jossey-Bass, 2012, 149–84.

33. This table is adapted from a table that appears in A. C. Edmondson. "Strategies for Learning from Failure." *Harvard Business Review* 89, no. 4, 2011.

34. S. Sitkin. "Learning Through Failure: The Strategy of Small Losses," in L. L. Cummings and B. Staw (eds.), *Research in Organizational Behavior* 14. Greenwich, CT: JAI Press, 1992, 231–66.

35. For the full Telco story, see A. C. Edmondson. *Teaming: How Organizations Learn, Innovate and Compete in the Knowledge Economy.* San Francisco: Jossey-Bass, 2012, 234–52.

36. A. C. Edmondson. "Phase Zero: Introducing New Services at IDEO (A)." Harvard Business Case 9–605–069, 2004; and A. C. Edmondson. *Teaming: How Organizations Learn, Innovate and Compete in the Knowledge Economy.* San Francisco: Jossey-Bass, 2012, 257–87.

37. A. C. Edmondson. *Teaming: How Organizations Learn, Innovate and Compete in the Knowledge Economy.* San Francisco: Jossey-Bass, 2012; and A. C. Edmondson. "Strategies for Learning from Failure." *Harvard Business Review* 89, no. 4, 2011.

38. T. Kelley and D. Kelley. "Reclaim Your Confidence." *Harvard Business Review*, December 2012.

39. A. C. Edmondson. *Teaming: How Organizations Learn, Innovate and Compete in the Knowledge Economy.* San Francisco: Jossey-Bass, 2012, 221–56.

40. Ibid., 26–27.

41. P. French. "Even People-Smugglers Have Ethics." *The Guardian* online, March 14, 2004. http://www.guardian.co.uk/theobserver/2004/mar/14/features.review37 (accessed June 21, 2013).

42. A. C. Edmondson. *Teaming: How Organizations Learn, Innovate and Compete in the Knowledge Economy.* San Francisco: Jossey-Bass, 2012, 240.

43. Ibid.

44. Ibid., 240–41.

45. A. C. Edmondson and L. Feldman. "Phase Zero: Introducing New Services at IDEO (A)." Harvard Business School Case 605–069, March 2013. (Revised from original February 2005 version).

46. E. Catmull. "How Pixar Fosters Collective Creativity." *Harvard Business Review*, 2008: 1–12.

47. See A. C. Edmondson. *Teaming: How Organizations Learn, Innovate and Compete in the Knowledge Economy.* San Francisco: Jossey-Bass, 2012, 171, for context; and *Fortune* for greater detail in A. Taylor III. "Fixing Up Ford." *CNNMoney* online, May 12, 2009. http://money.cnn.com/2012/11/01/autos/mulally-ford-succession.fortune/index.html (accessed June 21, 2013).

48. A. Taylor III. "Fixing Up Ford." *CNNMoney* online, May 12, 2009. http://money.cnn.com/2012/11/01/autos/mulally-ford-succession.fortune/index.html (accessed June 21, 2013).

49. A. C. Edmondson. *Teaming: How Organizations Learn, Innovate and Compete in the Knowledge Economy.* San Francisco: Jossey-Bass, 2012, 115–48.

50. Ibid., 149–84.

51. Ibid.

52. M. D. Cannon and A. C. Edmondson. "Failing to Learn and Learning to Fail (Intelligently): How Great Organizations Put Failure to Work to Innovate and Improve." *Long Range Planning* 38, no. 3 (June), 2005: 299–319.

53. R. S. Nickerson. "Confirmation Bias: A Ubiquitous Phenomenon in Many Guises." *Review of General Psychology* 2, no. 2, 1998: 175.

54. A. C. Edmondson. "Framing for Learning: Lessons in Successful Technology Implementation." *California Management Review* 45, no. 2 (Winter), 2003: 34–54.

About the Author

Amy C. Edmondson is the Novartis Professor of Leadership and Management at the Harvard Business School, a chair established to support the study of human interactions that lead to the creation of successful enterprises that contribute to the betterment of society. Edmondson joined the Business School faculty in 1996 and has taught courses in leadership, organizational learning, and operations management in the MBA and Executive Education programs. Her writings on organizational learning and leadership have been published in more than sixty articles in academic and management journals, and she has consulted widely on these topics for organizations around the world. In 2003, the

Academy of Management's Organizational Behavior division selected Edmondson for the Cummings Award for outstanding achievement, and in 2000, it selected her article "Psychological Safety and Learning Behavior in Work Teams" for its annual award for the best published paper in the field. Her article with Anita Tucker, "Why Hospitals Don't Learn from Failures: Organizational and Psychological Dynamics That Inhibit System Change," received the 2004 Accenture Award for significant contribution to management practice. She is the author of *Teaming: How Organizations Learn, Innovate, and Compete in the Knowledge Economy* (Jossey-Bass, 2012).

Before her academic career, she was director of research at Pecos River Learning Centers, where she worked with founder and CEO Larry Wilson to design and implement change programs in large companies. In the early 1980s, she worked as chief engineer for architect/inventor Buckminster Fuller, and her book *A Fuller Explanation: The Synergetic Geometry of R. Buckminster Fuller* (Boston: Birkhauser, 1987) clarifies Fuller's mathematical contributions for a nontechnical audience. Edmondson received her PhD in organizational behavior, AM in psychology, and AB in engineering and design, all from Harvard University. She lives outside Boston, Massachusetts, with her husband, George Daley, and their two sons.